ALL THINGS AT ONCE

ALL THINGS *at* ONCE

MIKA BRZEZINSKI

with
Daniel Paisner

WEINSTEIN
BOOKS

ISBN: 978-1-60286-111-4

First Edition
10 9 8 7 6 5 4 3 2

To my mother, the artist

Just be elegant.

—Emilie Benes (my grandmother)

CONTENTS

Mʏ ᴛʜᴀɴᴋs to Judy Hottensen and her colleagues at Weinstein Books, for believing in this project, and to Mel Berger at William Morris Endeavor, for helping me to get the word out and stay on point.

To Dan Paisner, who somehow found a way to do something I have never been able to do—organize my life, from beginning to end, collaborating with me to match the stories with a message we believe will resonate with women of all ages.

To Leslie, Beth, Jenny, Gina, and Jay, for their patience and encouragement along the way.

To SuSu for making all things at once even remotely possible.

And my greatest thanks to Jim, Emilie, and Carlie, for their unending support of Mommy.

COLD OPEN

October 30, 1998—Yonkers, New York

*H*ER TINY BODY *had gone limp.* "She's not moving!" *I screamed into the phone.* "The noises she's making are all wrong. It doesn't sound like her. And she's not moving at all, from her chest down!"

I could hear the alarm in our pediatrician's voice. "Mika," *she said firmly.* "You have to get her back to the hospital. Drive her yourself, if you can. We'll call ahead and get them ready for you."

I followed the doctor's orders, moving quickly, mechanically, all the time chanting, "Please make her okay, please make her okay." *Over and over. Pleasemakeherokay, pleasemakeherokay . . .*

I don't remember putting my infant daughter in her car seat or driving to the hospital. I have a vague memory of pulling in to the emergency room parking lot and flinging open the driver door. I know I left the engine running, and the car angled in the ambulance zone. It had barely been a half hour since we'd been to this same emergency room, since these same doctors and nurses had examined Carlie and told me she was okay. But they were wrong. We were met in the reception area by the same hospital worker who'd checked us in on our first visit, and now he was trying to put me through the same procedure all over again.

"Name?" he asked calmly. "Social Security number?"

I didn't have time for procedure. Carlie didn't have time. My doctor had called ahead, I explained. It had all been arranged. But I could not make myself understood, and now the mechanical fog that had gotten me to the hospital was lifting. I went from panic to confusion and finally to rage. Now all I could think was that this man and his forms were standing between my baby and the help she needed. He needed to get out of our way. I placed Carlie's car seat gently on the floor and flew toward him, grabbing his shirt and the skin on his neck. I dug in and told the attendant in the clearest language possible that his life depended on his ability to get out of the way. Out of Carlie's way. Then, in a swift, single movement, I rushed toward him and shoved him against the wall. As I did so, I flashed on an image of a mother summoning the strength to lift a car off her injured child. To me, it was a matter of life and death. I had to get my baby in there. Nothing would stand in my way.

From the corner of my eye, I could see one of the nurses reach for a phone—probably to call security. Then, another nurse stepped in as if to separate me from her colleague. She didn't have to. I saw her approach and let the man go. The nurse *saw me retreat and reached instead for Carlie—still in her car seat, still on the waiting room floor. In that moment the nurse must have seen they were up against the power of a mother's instinct. Or maybe the message from Carlie's doctor had finally reached the reception desk. It didn't matter which.*

Instantly, Carlie was surrounded by doctors, nurses, technicians. Some of them I recognized from before. But they were different now, all moving in the urgent choreography of emergency. I stood off to the side. I called my husband, Jim. He was on his way before I could finish my first sentence . . . but it was a Friday, and he was coming from the city, and it would take him forever.

I watched helplessly as doctors pressed a series of needles into Carlie's little toes, and got no response. She was awake and conscious, but she was completely unresponsive. I was still standing uselessly to the side when I heard someone whisper words that rang through my brain as if through a loudspeaker: "Spinal cord damage."

Everything got quiet and far away. Then I heard the words echo again: Spinal. Cord. Damage. If I hadn't been leaning against the wall, I would have melted to the ground. It was like being stuck inside one of those dreams where you want to scream but nothing comes out.

One doctor called a spinal cord expert at another hospital. "How soon can you get here?" I heard him say.

I watched as they rolled little Carlie into an adjacent imaging room for an MRI. All I could do was wait. I felt my knees go soft and my back slide farther down the wall as a terrible thought began to take shape: this was my fault. This didn't have to happen. We'd fallen down a flight of stairs, because I was exhausted. Because I was spent, distracted. Because I was practically sleepwalking with my baby in my arms, weighed down by my impossible schedule and worries of what lay ahead. One moment Carlie was in my arms, and then she wasn't. One moment I was on my feet, talking a hundred miles an hour to the sitter. The next, I was in a free fall, crashing down a full flight of stairs . . . bumping down hard, bouncing off the steps and up against the wall, unable to stop myself or my baby girl. When we'd finally crashed to the landing below, her tiny frame was pressed between me and the floor.

Now my four-month-old was in that imaging room, on the other side of the door, inside a giant metal machine, while I was slumped against the wall, reliving the horror of what had just happened to my precious baby girl. She was only a few months old, and I was supposed to take care of her. Nothing was more important. But at this moment all I was thinking about was how I had failed Carlie. How I let this happen. How I was to blame.

How could I have let myself get so run down, so exhausted at work that I would fumble over my own feet and fall down a steep flight of stairs with my newborn in my arms? It made no sense to me—and yet, here I was, waiting for word about what her life would look like now. Wondering if she'd ever be able to move. All for what? A blind ambition to be all things to all people? To be a super hockey mom?

After another beat or two, I could no longer stand against that wall. My legs crumbled beneath me, and I slid to the floor. At one point, I was looking at this pathetic scene of myself as if from above. I could see my face pressed against the cool, filthy linoleum of the hospital floor. I could see that I was weeping.

This was my rock bottom, and as I lay there I thought, How can I ever forgive myself for what I've just done?

Sometimes You Have to Take a Step Back

As a young girl, whenever I imagined my career, I always had an age-based "end date" for it all: forty. That was no target date or deadline by which I meant to have arrived at whatever job or place or purpose I'd set out for myself. No—that, to me, was the finish line.

After that, I'd be done. I'd retire into motherhood and the role of supportive wife, which I had always wanted to be at the center of my identity.

I knew early on that I wanted to be in television news—a business that is so visually oriented it naturally imposes a shelf life on the careers of most women, with only a few exceptions. I factored that in to my thinking and my plans. That might seem like a cynical or calculating view for a girl of sixteen or seventeen, but I considered myself a realist, even as a kid. I was steeling myself for the road ahead.

And, like clockwork, that's exactly what happened. When

I was thirty-nine years old, my career came to a halt, right on schedule. I walked out the front door of CBS News and thought, *Wow, I was dead on.* I went from the broadcast center up 57th Street to my parking garage, wondering the whole way how it was that I'd been so right about this and so wrong about so much else. What I hadn't planned on was how depressed and hopeless I would feel about the loss of my career. How such a big part of me would be wiped away. So that was one surprise. The other was that my timeline was all wrong. The end actually turned out to be only the beginning: a new jumping-off point in my professional journey and a chance to press the reset button and start all over—from the bottom, but this time with a whole new set of hard-won skills and absolutely no fear. It was an opportunity that would lead to where I am today: on the air for five hours a day, smack in the middle of the national conversation.

Maybe it was in my genes, or maybe it was my generation. But from the day I was born, like a lot of women who came of age in the 1970s and '80s, it was instilled in me that I could achieve anything I set out to accomplish. Nothing was out of reach. It was a mind-set handed down to me from my mother and grandmother, both brilliantly talented and highly resourceful women.

And yet as I notch my twentieth year in television news, a high-profile, high-stress, high-expectations field where our shortcomings as women and journalists and wives and mothers are brought to full and prominent attention, I'm starting to realize the lessons I took from my mother and grandmother were perhaps a little too thorough. Because of the hard work and sacrifice of trailblazers before me, there are indeed many more choices available to women of my generation. There are far fewer glass ceilings blocking our rise to the top of our chosen fields. But in addition to all these possibilities I'm starting to hear a new message. This one doesn't come from my mother, or grandmother, or any mentors I've collected on my journey, but from within. From me. A message I am still working to put in play before my children move on into adulthood: pace yourself.

Nothing more than a yellow caution light, but for me it is the most important lesson I can pass on to my own daughters. Go your own way. Narrow your focus. Breathe. It's what twenty years of running and gunning and "accomplishing" has taught me. It's not about slowing down, but strategizing for the long haul. Pull back when your gut says you should. Now that all these choices have unfolded for us, it's important for women to accept and expect them and sort through what needs to be accomplished when. And, by the way, motherhood should never be pushed down that list, if you mean to be a mother. We should stop being so pleasantly surprised at all these inroads we're making and start looking at them pragmatically. We need to time our career moves *and* our rites of passage carefully, which means making tough, clear decisions along the way.

Looking back, I realize my biggest failures always seemed to find me when I was trying to do too much too soon. When I wasn't ready to accept that I needed to choose one aspect of my life over another—or risk crashing and losing everything. Your job can be a big part of who you are, but it shouldn't be the whole package. Your family and relationships should be central, but they needn't be front *and* center at all times. I'll be the first to admit that I didn't always get that. I get it now. For a long time I was probably the last person on the planet in a position to talk about "having it all," slowing down, or seeking that fine balance between family and career. My husband and children would be the first to tell you that I failed to find that balance on many occasions. No question, I've made some painful miscalculations along the way. But it's because I've taken a close, tough look at some of those missteps that I'm able to walk a more certain road today. It's because of that effort and the support of my husband and children that the journey continues.

Now that I've enjoyed a level of success on *Morning Joe*, the daily news show I cohost on MSNBC with Joe Scarborough, many women I meet seem to want to focus on my unlikely career path. From reaching the upper echelon of CBS News, to being dumped by the network, to being unable to find a job *any-where* in television, to where I am now. And the more I talk about my own doubts and struggles, the more I assess my wrong-headed turns and my ill-considered career moves, the more I see how much they mirror the difficulties of other women.

Fortunately, I have done a few things right along the way: planning for career, marriage, and family, collectively and early on. I am enormously proud of the effort I put into assembling all these aspects of my life at a time when most of my peers believed they could put off marriage and children until their careers were established.

Motherhood is one of the first things I talk about when I speak with young women about jump-starting their career—even if they don't ask. "Don't forget to have children," I say. "If you want a family, don't put it off." I'll usually get some confused looks and bulging eyeballs in response—as in, *Did she just say* that? It's a message young women don't often hear, but I believe it's elemental. There's nothing wrong with putting both family and work at the top of your list of priorities, giving each equal value and care, right from the start. I'd even argue that finding a good man is far more difficult than finding the right job, and it's one of the most important decisions you'll make in life, so why put it off? If that's what you want, start reaching for it now. All of it. The sooner, the better.

The 2008 presidential election was a real eye-opener for me in this regard. Throughout the campaign, we were regularly visited on the *Morning Joe* set by women who were changing the career-marriage-family ideal by their powerful example. Our show was in its infancy, but we had quickly become an important stop for candidates on the road to the White House. We traveled from Iowa to New Hampshire and to almost every other state in the run-up to Super Tuesday, broadcasting live for up to six hours a day, on location, before jumping back on a plane and heading off for the next political battleground. Between road trips, the candidates came to us. The experience gave me a spectacular front-row seat to a compelling moment in our nation's history, as we elected our first African-American president, but more than that it allowed me to consider yet again the changing face of the American career woman. I was one of the first broadcast journalists to conduct an extensive interview with Michelle Obama, our future First Lady. I found her to be a magnificently intelligent and truly modern woman, one who balanced her career, her children, and her marriage with the struggle to break through subtle and not-so-subtle racial barriers—all with abundant grace and good cheer.

I admired Michelle Obama all the more once I admitted to myself that there had been times in my own life when grace and good cheer were in short supply. My own ambition and drive had sometimes caused me and my family great trouble and hardship. I used to feel guilty about every small success at work, because it pulled me from the joys and wonders unfolding at home; and I felt self-indulgent about time spent with my family, because it distracted me from my career. I wanted to see myself as a kind of superwoman, giving my all to my husband, my children, and my job at all times, but I could never seem to get it right. I moved about feeling like a salmon trying to swim up Niagara Falls.

For years I denied that reporting, storytelling, and performing on the air are a big part of who I am. Instead of celebrating that and focusing on it when appropriate, I rushed around plugging holes and trying to compensate for it and give everything else equal time. What I have finally learned is to embrace this part of my identity and redefine my other, equally important, roles. Sometimes, this means making difficult decisions. I might have to spend time away from our children. Their day-to-day needs might have to be met and managed by my husband, or my friends, or a hired caregiver while I take a sideline role.

Many working women grapple with this issue. "Giving up control" of the children, very often to a nonfamily member, is a big source of tension and stress in a lot of two-career households. Personally, I'm a bit of a control freak, and there were times when

I felt a little lost, knowing I was not fully in charge. And yet, over time, I learned that my kids are better off being with me when I can give them *all* of me. For a long time I tried to push ahead through tremendous exhaustion just to say that I could do it all. I wanted to show the world that I could manage a career with crazy hours, be a wife, run a household, and take care of small children. In the end—or, at least, in that end that found me at thirty-nine years old being cast off from CBS News—I saw that this was impossible. We all paid a price for that lesson.

Joy. Knowing who you are. Hitting the right notes, at the right time. This is the kind of *having it all* that my mother managed to capture years before me. She did things in her own way, in her own time. As a child, I watched her struggle as she and my father navigated through their conflicting interests. Like me, she knew at a young age what she wanted to do with her life. She wanted to be an artist. A sculptor. She had been an art history major at Wellesley, and taught art history at Boston College. She hadn't started exhibiting her own work just yet, but she was getting there. She took on the art world and all its challenges as well as marriage and three children. Her sense of self took a hit in 1976 when she was forty-four years old, just about the same age I am now, as I write this. She packed up her hopes and dreams and moved me, my brothers, the dog, the ducks, the cat, and the rabbit from New Jersey to Virginia, so my father could accept a job as President Carter's national security adviser and she could try on the unfamiliar role of dutiful Washington wife. She reminded us every step of the way what she was giving up. At times, she let us know loud and clear that she would rather be pursuing her art. Parts of her new life were utterly boring to her. Tedious. Frivolous. And it's only now that I appreciate the trade-off she made, between hearing her own voice and answering the call as a wife and mother—all equally important to her.

I get it now. I get that my mother was biding her time, pacing herself until she could achieve her goals. She was a proud and passionate and boundlessly talented woman taking a step back from her artistic dreams and signing on instead for the opportunity afforded my father and our family. It was a once-in-a-lifetime chance to embark on a truly unique adventure. The reality of my mother's situation was that she put a huge part of herself on hold, and hit that reset button for my father, for our family—and for our country. She was still an artist, but for four years she was an artist on pause, counting the days until she could hit that button again and put herself back in play. Even as a child, I could sense she was frustrated—like a racehorse stuck at the gate. She kept up with her work in fits and starts, but during that period she was constantly setting aside an essential piece of her identity, and then picking it back up again. In all that time, she never lost sight of her goals as an artist.

We finally talked about this, in a weirdly public way, after I had my own children, at a time when I thought I had it all figured out. I was sadly mistaken—deluded, really. I still thought I could do anything, be anything, overcome anything. More than that, I thought I *needed* to do all these things in order to be . . . well, *me*. I was working as a correspondent for CBS News. One of the great benefits of my time at the network was that reporters were encouraged to pursue stories of personal interest, and that kind of freedom led me to do a piece on my own mother for the Mother's Day edition of *CBS Sunday Morning,* with Charles Osgood. I went back home to Virginia with a crew and turned the camera on my mother, and what I got back was a revelation.

There in front of a vast audience my mother finally opened up about what that move to Virginia had really cost her all those years ago. And, crucially, I was finally open to hearing what she had to say. It took listening as a journalist and not just as a daughter for me to really hear her, and to figure out how her picture fit alongside mine. On that fine spring day, when I was coming into my own as a wife and mother and reporter and my mother was coming to terms with the choices she'd made as a younger woman, we reached a wonderful patch of common ground at my parents' mountaintop property in rural Virginia—a place where my mother's massive wooden sculptures peek out of the landscape. I think the camera helped, because we had the sense that we were pushing these buttons for the record. We'd talked around some of these issues before, but here it would matter. There would be others listening in. This time, my mother knew that I would have no choice but to pay attention, to get the story right.

"Be honest," I said, when we'd reached a point of pause in our discussion. "Do you see yourself first as a mother, a wife, or an artist?"

"Oh," my mother said, with her wonderful, strong European accent. "That is impossible to answer, because I am all those things at once."

"All things at once," I echoed, and for the first time I realized the sheer weight of my mother's dilemma nearly thirty years earlier. She kept so many plates spinning it's a wonder so few of them dropped, and a separate wonder she managed to keep them all intact. But it was only now, here, on this return trip to the place of my growing up, with a CBS News crew in tow, that I allowed myself to really hear my mother's story. There was no note of complaint in her voice. No tinge of regret. Just the bittersweet truth that one has to be patient. That we can't really have it all right away. Not in full measure. That takes time. Pacing. Determination. Strategy. A sense of self. And as I sat and listened, I realized for the first time that my mother had managed to find that perfect balance.

It had taken her fifty years, but she got there. While I was still very much a work in progress, lacking that same balance in my own life.

What I took away from this public exchange with my mother was that it's right and good and necessary to carry all these different pictures in our minds as we move on in the world, but it's also right and good and necessary to step back every once in a while and bring just one of those pictures into focus. To *see* everything you believe yourself to be, even if you can't *be* all those things all the time. She did that beautifully. I think of the fits and starts she endured as a younger woman, and the groove she seems to finally be in now, working in her studio every day. I picture her tirelessly preparing for her next big show—aptly titled "Family Trees." It's an expression of life, love, us. But mostly it's an expression of herself—fully realized.

Yes, we can *be* all things at once, my mother told me. In fact, we must. But we must also accept that we can't *do* everything all at once. It's about mapping out, navigating, and constantly renegotiating your career, marriage, and family plans. All equally important—and all, ultimately, at once.

ONE

The Secret Shapes of Trees

BEFORE WE WERE in the fishbowl of Washington politics, our family lived in relative obscurity in Englewood, New Jersey. It was a busy household. My father, Zbigniew Brzezinski, taught Soviet studies and foreign policy at Columbia University, where he headed the Institute on Communist Affairs. My mother, Emilie Benes Brzezinski, was an artist working to find her voice. Dad commuted into Manhattan while my mother worked in her studio in our basement. There was my eldest brother, Ian, and then my brother Mark, and then me. Active, disciplined, worldly people, my parents expected their children to keep pace. There were always big projects going on at our house. And there were always animals, which would inevitably lead to dramatic "disaster" scenes, like when the dog ate my rabbit, or the dog ate the neighbor's dog, or the neighbor's dog ate our ducks!

If you ask my mother, she'll say I was the hardest one to

raise. She had a point. Surrounded by two brilliant brothers and two wise and eccentric parents, I struggled to fit into our intense family dynamic. The bar was set fairly high in our household, and I'm afraid I didn't always rise to meet it. My father wrote important books and gave important speeches, and his world revolved around power and influence and being an expert on geostrategic relations. My mother, meanwhile, was an amazing artist, at that time working in plastics.

My parents worked to foster big ideas in each of us—ideas I couldn't always get my head around as a little girl. My brothers seemed to manage this more easily. Even at an early age, they seemed well on their way toward foreign policy careers of their own—one as a Republican and the other a Democrat, a sign of the freethinking that blossomed in our home. During the 2008 presidential election, Ian worked as a McCain supporter and Mark worked for Team Obama, with me navigating the middle in the rapidly changing world of television news.

From time to time the scene shifted to my grandmother's house next door. I spent almost every day there. My grandmother, also named Emilie Benes, made it a special point to cultivate me and to share the stories of her transcontinental life. My grandfather's uncle had been the president of Czechoslovakia, so my grandmother married into a family of prominence, and she made an effort to hold up her end. She spoke eleven languages and taught me one of them, French. She raised two sons and a daughter, my mother, ultimately on her own, which was a rare and brave thing in her day. She came to the United States by way of the U.S.S. *Hilary* during World War II. My grand-

father had been appointed as the consul general for Czechoslovakia, based in San Francisco, and together they packed their
three children with everything they could possibly wear and
carry and boarded the ship in Liverpool to cross the Atlantic. On
the way, the *Hilary* was hit by a torpedo. It failed to explode but
was lodged in the hull. It was a ticking time bomb, and everyone
had to abandon ship in lifeboats. My mother remembers seeing
other ships exploding across the water, lighting up the night sky.
The torpedo never exploded, and the crew was able to dislodge
it. My mother relives those moments as if they were yesterday.
She was only ten years old, but the images remain emblazoned
in her mind. My family then went west, and after educating their
children in California schools, my grandmother separated from
my grandfather and ended up running a retirement home—
among other business pursuits. As a single working mother with
three teenagers, she did well. Her two sons ended up at Harvard
and Princeton—and my mother went to Wellesley.

The great and abiding lessons of my grandmother's life, for
me, were to be proud, graceful, and resourceful. She had faith that
these traits could be found within me. When I overheard her
talking about me to other people, she always used the word
"clever." I liked that, even if I didn't know exactly what she
meant. She taught me to use all my talents to their full extent—
always, always, always reminding me of the importance of being elegant, an aspect of grace she came by naturally. Oh, and
while I was at all this, I had to practice my French. "Please learn
your French," she used to implore. And I did my best to comply.

To this day, I remain fairly fluent in French, but I have

little use for it—just the wonderful fact that it reminds me of my grandmother. When I was a little girl, my mother made the most amazing picture book for me about my two dolls, Raggedy Ann and Imogene. It was half French, half English. It's such a joy to read now. I had it rebound and printed and gave it to my daughters and my niece on Christmas, and it's become a cherished family keepsake for the way it connects us to my grandmother.

My grandmother was a huge influence on me well into adulthood. She was also a daily presence—that is, until I was nine years old, when my father came home from the city one evening late in 1976 and gathered us around. He said, "Congratulations, we're moving to Washington."

That's how we found out my dad had been appointed by President-elect Jimmy Carter as his national security adviser. It was a different world back then, far different from the information age we live in today, although at the time we all *thought* we were in an information age. We children were encouraged to read the newspaper, watch the evening news, and hold up our end of the family dinner table conversations on economic policy or foreign policy or politics in general. It wasn't just that we had to be well read; our opinions had to be carefully considered; most important, they had to be our own. We were always challenged to be aware of what was going on in the world, and we explored these developments every night over dinner. This particular piece of national news, however, was just dropped into our laps while we were standing on the landing in our upstairs hallway, and the next thing I knew we were moving.

It happened like wildfire. There was no time to worry about

how to adjust to our exciting new situation, because from that moment on, life became a series of such adjustments. In a flash, we were driving down to McLean, Virginia, where my parents had found an old run-down farmhouse on a five-acre piece of property. We packed and moved ourselves. Being a child of the Depression era, and taking up her own mother's example, my mother did everything in the cheapest, most difficult way possible. Everything. The farmhouse needed a lot of work, and we were on a budget, so we put up our own fence around the property. Pet geese came into the picture—chickens, too—so we had fresh eggs. Then, a pony named Strawberry. We built a stable for Strawberry—built it ourselves, of course, with my mother as head carpenter. And, symbolically, we cut our own trail through the overgrown woods behind our house. My mother the demon woodcutter had us out there like a team of sweaty, filthy, Slavic hillbillies, clearing our own land. We always seemed to have cuts and bruises all over our bodies. It was backbreaking work, but there was a purpose to it, a sense that we were all in this thing together. We learned what it felt like to accomplish a goal—even if it was set by someone else and involved forced labor.

Amy Carter was one of my first playmates after we moved. We were about the same age, so it made sense that we were thrown together, since our dads worked so closely. I went to the White House for playdates in the tree house on the South Lawn. Once, Amy and another "daughter of" dared me to drink a bottle of Tabasco sauce in her tree house. We were playing "truth or dare" and to me, "dare" was far better than "truth"—so I drank the whole thing, without flinching once. We even had sleepovers there, with other kids our age who were connected to the administration, or who went to school with Amy.

As a family, we went to all sorts of White House events and had the opportunity to accompany the First Family on Air Force One and Marine One. I slept over at Camp David as well. On one of my trips there, I asked Amy if I could drive the golf cart. I had no idea how to drive it, but she let me drive anyway. Bad move. I ended up bumping into Menachem Begin's shins. He was standing next to Anwar Sadat, which officially made this my first awkward moment with a world leader. There would be many, many others.

Rosalynn Carter was an attentive mother—and a proper, genteel southern woman who always thought my face was too dirty. It certainly was, and indeed that's the one memory of Mrs. Carter I carry with me, from all that time spent playing with Amy and visiting with the Carters: the First Lady chasing after me around the White House, trying to wipe my face clean. She was so warm, so welcoming, and I was always getting into some mess or other, like a regular Pig-Pen.

When I picture myself in those days, showing up at the White House, I was in secondhand clothes. I'd be surrounded by all these children from the administration, and they'd all be dressed to the nines, but I'd be in pants that were too short for me, or maybe my zipper wouldn't work. On top of that I wasn't much of a groomer, so if you see pictures of me from back then you won't mistake me for a child model for Ralph Lauren. I was a mess!

Apart from these frequent visits with Amy, my mother determined that we would not be like the other transplanted families who descended on the Carter White House. We would not be predictable in any way. She had made the move to Washington with defiance, on her own terms. There'd be a change of scenery, but she would keep her focus. She wouldn't be one of those cookie-cutter Washington wives of the period, who went to lunch and took up various causes to bolster their husbands' careers. She refused to give up her art completely, although it now fell to her to ferry us kids from school to our various activities and to take on a greater share of the household management in consideration of my father's round-the-clock schedule. But she continued to sculpt, spending what little free time she had carving thrilling and enormous pieces from downed trees she collected in the area. She used to tell us the trees held a secret shape inside of them, and she was just helping to bring it out with her chainsaw, chisel, and ax . . . whatever it took. In this way, and in so many others, my mom was so different from any of the other mothers I knew. As a kid, I defined "different" as "embarrassing." Today, "remarkable" comes to mind. She'd be hacking away at her sculptures, dirty from head to toe, and in a blink she'd throw off her workman's suit, bathe, put on lipstick and a ball gown, and rush off to a state dinner at the White House with sawdust in her hair.

Even when my father prevailed on my mother to host some visiting dignitaries, she did it in her own way. She grew her own vegetables and cooked her own meals. She didn't decorate her house like a page out of some fancy magazine, or dress her children like little dolls. Nothing about our lives was for display—except, of course, for my mother's sculptures. Our living room was filled with comfortable, mismatched furniture, collected from my parents' trips around the world—including many months in Japan—without us. We got a lot of our clothes second-hand. I remember wearing a pair of Sears Toughskins jeans, which we'd gotten from some local thrift store, and hoping no one would notice. It's not that my mother was cheap, just practical. To her thinking, used clothes were as good as new ones.

We always felt like the poorest kids in the upper-middle-class town of McLean, Virginia, but my parents knew we were rich in the ways that really mattered—with big ideas and unrivaled opportunities.

My father wasn't much help around the house. He's finally learned to make a cup of coffee, but that's about it. My mother took on much more around the house than he did, and she did it (mostly) without complaint. She might not have done it the way the other moms were doing it, but she had her own way. We weren't disgusting slobs, not by any stretch, but a messy kitchen never really bothered her. She might let the dishes pile up, but she was busy. She had things to do. And now that we were in Virginia, she had to be the statesman's wife, so there was this whole other layer of responsibility.

Looking back, I can't help but think she got the balance exactly right. As a kid, I used to be embarrassed that we didn't have the perfect home, or that we didn't have the nicest clothes, or that we stood out in any way. I used to tell myself, "I'm going to be a better mother." And now, my priorities are definitely more in line with my mother's than I ever would have thought while I was growing up.

When it came to entertaining, the convention around town was to hire fancy caterers and serving staff, and for the hosts to try to one-up or outdo each other, but that wasn't my mother. Not at all. She invited people into her home and presented our family as we were. There were animals everywhere, including a huge German shepherd that would terrorize the Secret Service. My brothers liked to hunt in the fall, so there was the occasional dead deer hanging from one of the trees. And at Christmas or New Years, just for a laugh, my mother would bring Strawberry the horse right into the house and have her sip vodka and beer with our guests. Once, Deng Xiaoping came for dinner and I spilled a plate of caviar on his lap. Another awkward moment. The leader of the People's Republic of China had a lapful of fish eggs, courtesy of me, a situation I made worse when I impulsively reached to brush it off with my hand. Cyrus Vance, President Carter's secretary of state, witnessed the whole thing, shaking his head. However notable, our visitors were meant to take us as is. Other Washington types would trot out their well-behaved kids to meet their distinguished guests, and then send them off to watch television in the basement or out with a baby-sitter, but not my parents. They put us to work. They made us serve dinner. They made us hang coats, mix drinks, and take it all in.

Another time, the socialite Pamela Harriman was expected at the house, along with a group of other dignified guests. My mother was a good and gracious host, despite her occasional protestations over having to host in the first place. She spent a lot of time thinking about what to serve, and making sure everything was just right. And as I said, she prepared everything herself. A couple of days before this particular dinner party, she happened to be driving to pick me up at school when she saw a dead deer by the side of the road. Naturally, she got out to check if the carcass was still warm. It was. So she started hacking it up right there. At first she thought she would just cart it back intact and string it up on one of the trees like my brothers did with their kills, but roadside butchering seemed easier. Some guy in a truck pulled over and helped her, and they ended up splitting the deer, and she brought her half home in the trunk of her car, thinking about how she might prepare it for her guests. To her, this was normal. She was a mess by the time she picked me up at school, about a half hour late, but I knew not to be surprised by anything where my mother was concerned. In fact, I knew if her workman's suit was covered with blood, some poor deer or wild turkey had seen its last day.

Mom was and is a wonderful, resourceful, and courageous cook, and she especially liked to cook venison, so she counted herself lucky to have stumbled across this great find. It was like winning some wild-game lottery. When Mrs. Harriman and company sat down to dinner, they took turns marveling at the venison, saying things like, "Mmmm!" "Delicious!" "Simply divine!" They wondered aloud who the caterer was, and where my mother got her venison.

Mrs. Harriman was just bringing her fork to her mouth when my mother blurted out her response. "Oh," she said, "I found it on Old Dominion Road. It had been hit by a car just moments before I pulled up! Isn't it wonderful?" She said this with genuine excitement. She could have been saying, "Oh, I got my shoes at Bloomingdale's, and they were 50 percent off! Aren't they *fabulous*?" She went on with her story, as mouths dropped all around the table. "I couldn't believe my good luck," she continued. "I gutted the thing right there, and skinned it, and brought the best part home for my guests."

I used to wince at what I perceived to be the "disconnect" between my mother and high society. Today, I celebrate it. The Brzezinskis were different, that's all.

What happened next was like a spit-take scene from an old *Honeymooners* episode. Pamela Harriman—midbite, mid-sentence—spit her mouthful onto her plate and turned ashen white. This proud, grand, refined woman, who had been married to Winston Churchill's son, who had dined at the finest restaurants and banquets and receptions all over the world, who would go on to become the U.S. ambassador to France, was simply aghast. And my mother, God bless her, couldn't understand the commotion. The story made the gossip section of the newspaper. Something about the Brzezinskis serving roadkill.

To this day, my mother has no idea what she did to cause all the fuss. Again, a disconnect—but one that allowed her to live on her own terms, in her own way, without worrying about what others might think. I know how hard that can be, to stay true to yourself under such scrutiny. I always admired my father's reaction to my mother in these circumstances, and here he was stoic, totally unfazed. This was his wife; he knew whom he had married. He wasn't at all surprised or ashamed. In fact, I think he was secretly proud of her.

It wasn't just Washington society that didn't quite know what to make of us. I tried to fit in at my new school, which wasn't so easy, with the Secret Service in tow at times, and other kids knowing I was a "daughter of." Often, I'd try to compensate for these two strikes against me by being overly nice and solicitous and accommodating, eager to make friendships and personal connections that had nothing to do with my family name. But then I'd bring some of my new friends home from school, and there'd always be something or other to undermine my extra efforts. A cluttered kitchen, say, with a mess of art projects and supplies, and wild-game gutting, and dinner ... all under way at the same time. It wasn't always so easy to make new friends. Once, I invited a girl to the house. She was the coolest girl in the school, with her blond hair and long legs. All the boys liked her. She came home with me one day after school, and I caught myself thinking, *This is going well.* Then she asked to use the bathroom, so off she went to the guest bathroom, just beyond the kitchen. A beat later, I heard a shrill, gut-wrenching scream. I'd forgotten that my mother had placed a dead deer in the bathtub, and opened the window so the carcass would stay cold until she had a chance to butcher it. Her plan was to do this last part in the kitchen sink, but by then my popular playmate was long gone—never to return.

The chickens and geese added full farm ambience to the place, which every year was surrounded by more and more McMansion-style houses. I adopted one of the chickens as my personal pet—a black one named Rose. I used to carry her around with me, everywhere, even while I was riding my pony. I'd go with my friends to the 7-Eleven down the street, and there'd be Rose, peeking her head out from underneath my coat, taking in the scene.

The geese helped, too, in their own way. My mother had purchased the pair to assist with her weeding. Lem and Lucious—our family pets and garden workers. I don't know how my brothers came up with those names, but these two white geese had the run of the place, so much so that one afternoon, on my way home from school, I saw a white goose in the middle of the road. I grabbed her by the neck and put her under my arm and carried her home, thinking she was one of ours. Turned out she wasn't, which was incredibly strange, because the chances of coming across a white goose in the middle of Old Dominion Road were about the same as finding one in midtown Manhattan.

Lem and Lucious certainly knew *me*, though. They were in the habit of wobbling out to greet me when I came home from school—and hissing, too—until one day when they didn't. I didn't give it much thought, until my brother Mark came chasing after me, baiting me in an especially taunting voice. He wanted me to know something was up. He said, "Hey, Mika. Where's Lem and Lucious? You *looking* for them?"

I said, "Ummm . . . yeah . . . where are they?"

Mark was enjoying this, so we went back and forth for a while, until he finally said, "They're hanging out back." Then he said it again, for emphasis: "*Hanging. Out.*" Like there were big quotation marks around the words.

I finally went to look for them—and there they were, *hanging out back*. From a tree. Upside down and headless. My mother had turned on them, tired of all the droppings underfoot. Lem and Lucious were done . . . or, dinner.

If there had been such a thing as reality television back then, we Brzezinskis would have been stars—a mix of the Osbournes and the Addams Family, in English with Polish subtitles. One episode would have been about our last-minute

25

invitation to have dinner with Pope John Paul II—an exclusive, private dinner with His Holiness and a few cardinals. It was set up because my father was one of the more prominent Polish Americans, but like everything else in our hectic lives, it was a last-minute deal. It really was an amazing experience, to visit with such a great man so intimately, but it was all we could do to fit it into our busy schedules. In fact, my brother Ian didn't want to go. He was sixteen at the time, and he actually refused to attend at first. He said, "I'm going to the friggin' football game. I'm not going to dinner with the friggin pope."

My poor mother had to pull three different teenagers from three different schedules and two different schools and do what she could to see that we were ready by the time the car came to pick us up. Ian wasn't helping with his rebellion—and to be fair, Mark and I were no picnic either. There wasn't time to see that we were all dressed appropriately. Ian, in a small act of defiance, arrived at the dinner in dirty hiking boots with un-tied laces, and ripped, filthy jeans. My father was already there when we walked into the dining room at the embassy, and he flashed my mother this cutting, disbelieving look that seemed to say, "How could you?"

There was nothing my mom could do but shrug her shoulders.

Pope John Paul II was such a warm, kind man he couldn't help but pick up on this little piece of tension between my parents, so he used his papal charms to smooth things over. He approached my mom and took her hand. Then he looked at my brother, and then back at my mother. Then he winked at her. It was the simplest, smallest gesture, but without a word he'd set my family at ease, and we ended up having the most wonderful, most spirited evening. Even Ian didn't seem to mind it in the end. At one point, while standing and talking to my dad, the pope reached over and pulled me close to him and kissed the top of my head, and it felt to me like I was inside one of my grandfather's hugs. There was warmth and good cheer all around—until my mother began to feel so comfortable with this great man that she started to challenge him with her opinions on birth control and other matters. My parents were like that. It was all about the discussion with them, the exchange of ideas. Life was one great big debate. Nothing was out of bounds. I don't think my father was too happy with my mother for pursuing this particular topic of conversation, but what could he say? We'd all been taught to be freethinkers, and to speak our minds, and she was doing just that.

My parents were able to help us recognize the richness and fullness of our lives, but I was still a challenge to cultivate. My older brothers didn't exactly help; they were a tough act to follow. They engaged like naturals at the dinner table, participating in fierce debate with my parents—usually to the great delight of my parents and their occasional guests. I was the youngest and felt like I couldn't keep up. I did find a role in helping "balance" discussions that seemed to go too far, when emotions ran high. I became the diplomat who helped bring opposing sides to common ground. I'd make a neutralizing comment. A joke to lighten the mood. Or, when needed, full-scale, hard-core diplomacy. Whatever it took to keep or restore the peace. And I would continue on in this role among my family as I got older—never comfortable as the main contributor, always the mediator.

I loved watching the psychological dynamics of a good intellectual fight between two or more big egos—although occasionally I'd be called on to offer an opinion of my own and I'd have to scramble. In television news, we call this "vamping," or "stretching." On the *Morning Joe* set, our stage manager Tim Bender makes the "stretch" motion with his hands when we have to fill time until the control room can catch up to us. I'm good at this—from all that practice around our family dinner table. Back then, whenever I was called on to speak at a table full of people, I'd make some small, sideline observation and hope it would be good enough to move the attention off me and onto one of the bigger egos. One thing I had going for me was that I was quick on my feet. I was funny—or, at least, I thought I was funny. One of my best little-kid jokes lived on . . . until my dog ate it: my rabbit, Bunny Sadr, named after Abolhassan Bani-Sadr, the first president of Iran after the 1979 revolution.

To my credit, I was more aware of the world around me than most children, but my parents expected more out of me than coming up with cute names for our family pets. They wanted their children to share their thirst for knowledge and achievement. In eighth grade, for example, I made the mistake of coming home with blue eye shadow and a comb tucked into my back pocket, looking pretty much like every other eighth-grade girl at the time. I was met with a freezing cold and violent hose-down, and after that my parents pulled me from the public schools of Langley, Virginia, and enrolled me at the Madeira School, an all-girls boarding school in town. There was no discussion. It was a swift and jarring change. I was a day student, so I wasn't uprooted from hearth and home, but I was separated from all my friends and from my routines. And boys were removed from the picture—no need for that eye shadow anymore, thank you very much. It was also a big academic challenge. I went from above-average grades in public school to Cs and Ds and worse. I had to take algebra twice, and counted every C+ as a moral victory, while my parents winced at every report card and searched endlessly for ways to make me a better student.

Try as I might, I just couldn't keep up with my brothers. They were excellent students. They ran track, too, so for a while I tried running—along with riding, which had quickly become my first love. After Strawberry, there were two other horses before I finally hung up my riding boots. I was always heading off to shows and competitions and lessons, and my mother dragged me and my horses all over the place. I don't know how she did it, because she wasn't just chauffeuring me and Strawberry, but Mark and Ian, too, to wherever they needed to be. Plus, she was back and forth to Madeira all the time for conferences with my teachers, trying to get a read on her underachieving daughter. It's a wonder she found any time at all to pursue her art, but she did—not, perhaps, in the full-on ways she'd imagined as a younger woman, but in whatever ways she could. She and my dad were very much partners, moving through life on their shared journey. This was his time, she believed. Her time would come soon enough. My mother was ever trying to widen our horizons—by mixing education with family fun and travel to exotic places—where we had to learn both history and geography. And so (when I was 14) we were the first non-Chinese (with Deng's special permission and a large escort) ever to retrace part of the Long March in the inaccessible Himalayan plateau of China; we visited the exotic parts of inland Morocco as guests of the king; we sweated through Luxor in Egypt—and then we were required to write essays on the experience.

I admire my father for recognizing that his marriage was a partnership between two individuals. He held up his end of the deal. When money poured in more freely after the White House years, he built my mom a massive studio on our property, and to this day she walks out her kitchen door, down a few steps built into the landscape, and across a bridge to open a door and step down into her world. Her studio is as big as a four-car garage—three stories high—with a winch that can drag in two-thousand-pound objects and hold them in the air while she carves away. It's really a magical place, filled with sculptures and tools and piles of sawdust and wood chips. There's a wood stove for warmth . . . and lots of mice. Visitors have to watch their step because my mother leaves cocked mousetraps all over the floor. She loves it in there. She spends morning, noon, and night there—payback for four years well served.

These days, my mother spends her time—full-time—doing to trees what she used to do to us. Looking for their secret shapes and revealing them to the world.

For the most part, it was an oddly idyllic childhood. Growing up in a farmlike setting? Surrounded by all manner of remarkable people? Sleeping in the White House tree house? Amazing. Occasionally, though, there'd be a shock of real-world clarity to bring me back to earth. One terrible experience taught me many lessons far too early, but it also proved to me that I had a resilient spirit.

It found me on horseback, when I was thirteen years old. Strawberry lived in the stable we'd built on our property, but for lessons I took her to the horse stables down the road. It was only a mile or so from our house, along Old Dominion Road, one of the busier, more traveled roads in McLean. The routine, for a while, was that I would ride her there on my own, after school or on weekend afternoons, and then I would ride her home. There was a footpath some of the way, but for about a half mile I'd ride on pavement on the busy two-lane road. After that, I'd walk Strawberry alongside a housing development and then across the street to Brook Valley Lane, where I'd duck onto a back road and some trails that took me straight to the horse farm. Whenever I crossed a street, I'd get off the horse and walk her, but I rode her the rest of the way, bareback.

Getting back on was never easy, with no good place to mount. Sometimes, when I'd try to climb back aboard Strawberry after crossing the street, it would take me a couple of jumps, but never more than a try or two. On this one occasion, while I was still on Old Dominion Road, I had such a difficult time of it that I didn't even notice when a man approached and lifted my legs and helped me up. Just some guy, out jogging. I didn't think anything of it. I said, "Thank you very much."

He said, "You're welcome."

I rode off and ducked onto that back road to take me the rest of the way, but as soon as I was out of sight of the main road the

31

man returned. I was completely surprised, but not scared just yet. He approached from behind, yelling for me to stop. At first I thought maybe I'd dropped something, and he was just running us down to return it. "Hey," he said. "Stop!" Not in a menacing way; his tone was actually friendly, helpful. So I brought Strawberry to a halt. Then when I turned I saw that the guy was holding a gun to my horse's neck. The guy dug the nose of the gun right into Strawberry's mane. It made no sense to me. I thought, *Who points a gun at a horse?* What could he possibly want? I didn't know what to do.

"Get off your horse or I'll shoot it," the guy demanded. His tone had gone from friendly to nasty in a blink.

I said, "Please don't kill my pony." He'd put that image in my head with his threat, and now that was all I could think about.

He said, "Then get off the damn pony."

I said, "What do you want? What're you going to do to her?" I couldn't imagine.

He said, "I'm not going to do anything to your pony." Then he said he just wanted to see me naked—specifically, he used a slang term for female genitalia that I had never heard before. I thought he was talking about my cat.

This threw me, for a beat. Not in a terrifying sort of way, but in a confusing sort of way. On some level I knew this guy wanted to hurt me. Somewhere in my mind, I knew he wanted to rape me, but I'd never heard this slang term before and it puzzled me.

I almost said something stupid like, "That's not a cat, that's my horse."

But then, of course, I knew. It just came to me: *No, Mika, you idiot, he's not after your cat.* I still wasn't processing exactly what he was after, but at the same time I also knew that I didn't want to go there in my mind. My thoughts were racing. I began to shake uncontrollably. My taut leg muscles, holding me upright on my pony, turned to jelly. My spine went limp, and I felt numb and cold.

I started to lose my hold on Strawberry. And then I thought the bad guy might shoot her, so I tried to grab on tight, but my attacker yanked me off and started beating me with his gun. On my face, my neck, my back. He was out of control, relentless. I felt nothing as it was happening, but I could hear the gun handle making tiny tapping sounds against my cheekbones. It was the strangest thing: I could *hear* it, but I couldn't *feel* it . . . as if my brain was protecting me. Or maybe this was just sheer terror, in full force, keeping me from the worst of it.

Strawberry galloped away in fear, and I was left on this dirt road, separated from the backyards of a row of houses by thick woods. It was late afternoon. Normally, I could see kids playing in those yards, through the trees. One of my classmates lived in one of those houses. Her little sister was always outside, playing with her friends. I screamed and shrieked wildly. The kids would hear me, I thought, but on this day there was no one. Not a single person could hear me—a cruel joke.

I screamed. It was the only way I could think of to fight back. I screamed and kicked as my attacker tried to drag me down into a ditch and rip my clothes off. He beat at me, and pulled at me, but I kept kicking wildly and spitting and screaming loudly. I was determined to prevent this man from getting what he wanted. I should have been afraid of the gun, but I was more focused on the way he said he would assault me. Whatever it took, I was not going to let it happen. And so I did the only thing I could: make as much noise as I possibly could, in such a way that I would scare him, call attention to him, frustrate him. But it only seemed to make him more violent.

And then, there came a moment when I was completely powerless and out of options, and we were face to face. Just me and my attacker. Close. Looking into each other's eyes. Out of moves, out of options. So I played the only hand I had. I said, "My father works in the White House! You don't want to do this! You do not want to do this. He will bring you down!"

I'd never done that before in my life. In fact, I had always gone the other way, never wanting to take advantage of my father's position or call attention to it. I worried constantly about putting myself in line for any kind of special treatment, but I wanted this guy to think it was too much trouble to mess with me. I wanted him to think he'd picked on the wrong little girl— a total desperation move, but I wanted to place a big doubt in his head, and what I came up with was to put it out there that I would unleash the full force of the United States government on him. And here's a strange thing: even as I was saying this to him I was thinking, *Wow, I never do that!*

The entire attack lasted no more than five or six minutes— hardly enough time for my mother to start worrying what was taking me so long. The plan was for her to meet me at the stable, which was what we always did, and I remember feeling like I was going to be hopelessly late. The attack, when I was in the middle of it, seemed to stretch on forever and ever.

At any rate, my "influence peddling" didn't work. So I kept screaming and kicking, hoping like hell someone in those nearby houses would hear me. Somehow, deep inside, I knew that I would find my way out of this situation. I made sure to get a good look at this guy's face. I wanted to be able to identify him. I wanted to make him pay later, in whatever ways I could. I burned his face into my memory. In the meantime, he beat me. But he couldn't shut me up, and he couldn't control my legs. As I fought back, I kept hearing my mother's voice in my head, with her thick accent: "Kick him between the legs! Kick him between the legs!"

Then suddenly I could see in his eyes that I'd done my job. He was spooked or disgusted or both, and probably now worried someone would hear me. He backed away and took off. Even after he left I couldn't stop screaming. It's like my body was on some kind of autopilot—in full-tilt, high-pitch, throat-tearing shriek mode. I got up and tried to pull myself together, but I was still screaming. I could see Strawberry, off in the distance. She was worried about me, I could tell. She hadn't gone very far, just a little ways down the path, and she kept inching closer and closer, walking back to me, but every time she got close, my screams scared her away. I had this little fight with myself, trying to get myself to stop screaming, because I needed Strawberry. At least, it felt to me at the time that I needed her. The very bad man was long gone, but I just couldn't stop. It was as frightening to me as the attack itself. I was inside the moment and outside it, all at the same time, and I couldn't make my body do what I wanted it to do.

Finally, after several minutes, I was hyperventilating, but

I wasn't screaming. When she drew near, I tried to talk to Strawberry in my most patient voice. I said, "It's okay. Everything's going to be okay." Like I was calming her down, even though what I was really doing was calming myself.

I tried to climb back on her, but kept sliding off—I was still limp and weak and shaking. Eventually, I found a tree stump and used it as a booster. I pointed Strawberry toward Shadybrook Stables, and we galloped. I cried. Loudly. Along the way, I could see people in their backyards and out by the path, and I shouted to them. I said, "Get back in your house. There's a crazy man loose. Get back in your house. There's a rapist!"

I must have looked like a lunatic, galloping along that path, my face all bloodied, my eye swollen shut, terrorizing these little children playing in their yards. Somehow by the time I got to the barn, about five minutes later, the police were already there. One of the kids playing in her backyard told her father that I'd galloped past, screaming and bloodied, and he alerted the police. I had no idea how long I'd been down in that ditch, how long this guy had been beating up on me, but now all these other wheels had been set in motion in such a way that all these people were waiting for me at the barn. My mother took one look at me and her face fell.

Strawberry was pretty spooked, and fairly thrashed. I had her galloping at such a clip someone needed to walk her for about an hour after we got to the barn to settle her. I took some settling, too. The police had a lot of questions, but I wasn't completely processing the magnitude of what had happened. Or what might have happened. Instead, I focused on what my mother was going through, seeing me like this. Also, I felt sorry for my riding teacher, who owned the barn. I didn't want anyone to get bad press.

The story did make the newspaper, but my name was kept out of it. They withheld some of the other details, too. The incident was widely reported, and a general warning was issued along with a description of the perpetrator, and that was where it ended—at least, on the public front. Privately, there were some ripples. My brothers were fuming, that someone could attack their kid sister in this way. They started driving around town looking for the guy. My father was outraged, too, and for a while he went out looking for him as well. My mother and I had to calm them all down, but it gnawed at everyone that the attacker was at large. It was an attack on all of us.

My mother slept in my bed with me that night—I think as much for her benefit as for mine. She needed to keep her baby close. She also needed me to need her, although I'm afraid I didn't quite need her the way she wanted. Not because I was brave or strong, but because I was too young to really understand what had happened. I knew about rape, but only on a surface level. I understood the danger I'd been in, but only on that same surface level. For the most part, what had registered was the physical assault. My brothers used to beat me up all the time, but not like that! My brothers had guns, but they'd never pointed one at me. This was far, far worse than anything my brothers had ever pulled, but when I broke it down, nothing about the situation was all that alien to me. So I processed it all in a very surface way and moved on from it as quickly as I could. My face healed, and I forgot about being scared on back roads. It was only later, when I got around to putting two and two together in a more adult manner that I allowed the true terror of those moments to fully register.

In many ways, the terror of that afternoon took its time sinking in. At first, all I knew was that this man wanted to hurt me. I felt scared, violated, and threatened in every way while it was happening, and then by the time I was back on my horse the word *rape* had finally slithered its way into my brain. It just landed there, without me fully realizing that this was what had nearly happened. I knew the word, and what it meant, but it wasn't part of my vocabulary. It was there, deep down, but I guess that's where I was, after everything that had happened . . . *deep* down. I caught myself screaming to all these little kids in their backyards that there was a rapist on the loose, because what else was I going to say? It surprised me when it came out of my mouth.

Somewhere in here was a lesson I wasn't quite ready to take in. Over time, I realized what this man was trying to do to me, and it led me to start thinking about what he almost took away from me. That's how my little-girl mind eventually processed the attack. It was something about power, and something about giving of myself, and I just wasn't going to be giving that to anyone—or letting them "take" it from me. Not until I was good and ready. And, as a Catholic, my resolve was backed by my religion.

About a week after the attack, we got word that a man matching my attacker's description had raped and brutalized a woman in the same neighborhood. A few weeks after that, there was another attack. And then another. Soon the local media had dubbed this bad guy "the jogger." Twenty years later, while I was working at MSNBC, the McLean police tracked me down and asked if I could identify a suspect. They'd found someone in Florida molesting children, and for some reason matched him up to "the jogger," so I drove down to Virginia for the lineup, and I went back to the scene, with the police, to the very spot where it happened. Now, as the mother of two little girls, my perspective was completely different. Now, as if for the first time, I was terrorized for the little girl I had been. And now this guy's face, which I'd spent those eternal minutes trying to memorize, was back in my head, doing a number on me. I closed my eyes, and there he was. I could see his eyes, still, but I couldn't spot him in that lineup. The guy was never found.

When Jimmy Carter lost the 1980 presidential election to Ronald Reagan, it meant my world was about to change yet again, only here the reset button wasn't so hard to push. As far as we kids could ever tell, my parents never really considered moving back to New Jersey. We'd made a life in Virginia, and that's where we would stay. What changed, really, was the way the world now looked back at us, once my father left the administration. Some of these changes were obvious and jarring: the red phone was ripped out of the wall at home; the Secret Service detail that had occasionally been assigned to us was gone. Other shifts were less tangible, like the way certain friends and status-conscious acquaintances disappeared from the picture, now that the spotlight pointed in a whole new direction. And it happened overnight. It was as if the people who had fawned and fussed over us for the past four years just evaporated.

My parents had warned us this would happen. We'd been told not to trust all the attention while we were in the middle of it, so once our position changed we didn't miss it. My father repositioned himself in Washington, and soon was off making speeches, advising the next administration and foreign governments as well through his home base at the Center for Strategic and International Studies. My mother dove back into her art. She'd already staged her first show, about a year or two into our Washington sojourn, but now she was able to pursue her work in a full-on way, including a major showing at the Corcoran Gallery of Art in Washington, DC, that really launched this next phase of her career. It seemed to me, looking on, like a seamless reset, with the focus shifting only a little. Their marriage would be renegotiated—but at this stage in their lives it was mostly fine-tuning. And because of my father's still high-profile position, that fine-tuning would still happen on a relatively public stage.

The sea change in how people saw them and the place they held in others' estimation might have derailed lesser people, but my parents are not lesser people. It was to be expected, they said. They laughed it off, and helped us to consider the triviality and ridiculousness of the entire political scene. Fame and influence are fleeting things, we were reminded at these new turns, and we would bend but not break in the shifting winds.

A few years later, there was some talk over the dinner table of my father running for the presidency of Poland. A group of Poles wanted my father to consider it, and he did for a moment, but he believed he had disqualified himself from a political future back home by living in the United States all these years and making his reputation here. He believed that to go back and run would cast him as a fake, a carpetbagger. Others wanted him to consider a run for the U.S. Senate. He was mulling his various options, but his supporters always failed to consider my mother in the equation.

Mom heard all this talk and said, "Nope, it's my turn."

She was firm on this. She'd put her own ambitions on hold so my father could sign on as national security adviser. For her it had been four years of waiting, being a supportive partner, and missing out on all kinds of opportunities to show her work. Now it was time to set right the pendulum. Now it was time for my father to fall in behind *her*.

My parents actually talked about these issues, in simple, blunt terms over dinner. They wanted us kids to be in on the conversation—not because we would have a say in the outcome, necessarily, but because they wanted us to experience the process and consider the options. Remember, it was all about the conversation in our house, and this was the topic of the moment.

It was impressed on me and my brothers early on that we were meant to have goals. Our parents never wanted us to waste time in front of the television. They wanted us to be active participants in whatever arena we chose. They wanted us to always challenge ourselves. At bottom, that's what most of these conversations were about—setting and meeting goals. My first career goal was to be a television news reporter. It was a natural extension of my experiences growing up, although it's interesting that my brothers had some of the same experiences and leaned toward foreign policy—and toward opposite political parties, no less. We were always going with my father to interviews and meetings and events. He liked bringing us along, because it was a good opportunity for us to spend time together. It also gave us a wonderful glimpse behind the curtain, to see how the world really worked. We went with him while he was interviewed on *Nightline, Today, Meet the Press*. While my brothers might have been listening to my father's carefully considered opinions, I was struck by the cameras, the lights, the producers . . . I wanted to know exactly what these television news people were doing, and how what they were doing led to what I was used to watching at home.

In our house, if you saw something you wanted you reached for it. So I started reaching. By the time I was fifteen, I was working as an intern at Channel 9, the CBS affiliate in Washington, DC, learning my way around a local newsroom. By sixteen, I was hosting my own cable-access show with my friend Melissa, *The Mika and Melissa Show*. As I recall, Melissa had a really large chest, so even then I took in the message that appearances count in television news.

I chased down every opportunity I could find. By the time I started college, I'd interned at every station in DC. The more I hung around, the more I learned, and the more I realized that this would be my career. I also realized it would take tenacity, luck, and a thick skin, but that just made me want it all the more. I liked that it would be relentless, unpredictable—nothing like a typical nine-to-five job. Plus, I liked the whole *production* of television news. I liked the reporting and writing and *assembling* of a story. I liked the thought of putting my voice and my personality and my worldview into my work. I liked how the best broadcast journalists found a way to get their stories across, to help people understand an issue or a trend or an event in a way that might have been out of reach. It was, for me, the perfect extension of the conversation that began around our family dinner table—the perfect segue from the role I played in our household while I was growing up to the role I have today, on the set every morning, keeping the conversation going.

TWO

Adventures in Television

T HE FIRST THING I learned when I graduated from Williams in 1989 was that my name would take me only so far. Perhaps if I'd wanted to be a diplomat, it would have opened a few more doors. But not in local television. I traveled up and down the East Coast, in and out of the smallest television markets, résumé in hand and begging for a chance to show some station manager what I could do. What they wanted to know was whether I could write a V-O (a voice-over read to go with video footage). Could I make "beat checks" (calls to cops, greasing them for tips)? Or could I cut and edit an S-O-T (sound-on tape)? No, I couldn't, so I was useless. The message was always the same: come back in a few years.

I'd had my own cable-access show in high school. I'd had my own show in my college town, too. I'd worked as an intern at every network, every summer since high school. I'd worked as a page on Capitol Hill. And I had my brand-new B.A. degree from Williams College. I thought I had everything covered.

I'd always assumed I'd have to start small and work my way up, but even starting small requires a break or two. And, in the days before round-the-clock news and information outlets on cable and the Internet, there weren't many jobs to go around. No one cared where I went to college, or who my father was. In fact, I think my pedigree bred resentment, if it came up at all. What small-market news directors wanted to know was if I could cover a fuel spill, or a fatal car crash, or a murder-suicide in the suburbs. Clearly, I was unqualified. So much so that I got only one job offer in the months just after graduation—at a teeny, tiny station in Vermont, on one teeny, tiny show meant to raise awareness on poverty. The pay? One hundred dollars for the show—that's it. I took the job for the chance to get a tape of myself on the air. That was the only reason. I'd already been turned down by a station in the smallest television market in the country—Presque Isle, Maine—so I guess you can say this Vermont job was big time. I moved all the way to Burlington and took a part-time, six-month job in the governor's press office in Montpelier to help pay the bills, just so I'd have that precious tape I could present to stations around the country. Just to put my one-and-only on-air piece on an audition reel that might or might not land me my next job. In my fantasies, news directors would watch the tape and think I was fabulous. In reality, I was not. When the red light went on, the overly dramatic makeup I'd applied myself started to drip. Badly. I sweated bullets. The hot lights mixed with the stress—

this was my one shot at a tape, and since it was a live broadcast there'd be no fixing it. It was horrific—a caricature. And it wasn't just how I looked. I was "acting," not reporting. Totally disconnected from the information I was trying to deliver. I was there for the wrong reasons.

I got my tape, but it was useless—unless you wanted a good laugh.

In fact, my entire Vermont sojourn was pretty much a waste. From the press office tour of duty to my "live" hundred-dollar show. I drove myself home to Virginia in my old Nissan Stanza, depressed. I was a failure on so many levels. This wasn't a career, I allowed myself to think. I'd wanted to be actively engaged in building my career, and laying the foundation for a family—and I was nowhere. I was going backward. Other women my age may have been thinking only about their careers at this point, or finding a relationship, but I'd always intertwined the two in my mind. After all, what is one without the other?

To borrow a line from Pat Buchanan that he shared one day on *Morning Joe*, I felt like "a big nothing-burger."

It was time to step back and regroup—the first time of many. I ended up taking the first *way* behind-the-scenes job I could find, working the overnight shift as a lowly assistant at ABC for *Good Morning America* and *World News This Morning with Mike Schneider*. The hours were murder, the responsibilities were negligible, and the pay was lousy—two hundred dollars per week, with no benefits because I was freelance. About the only thing I learned during my time at ABC News was what I *didn't* want to do—namely, work overnights. I vowed I would never, never, *never* work such horrible hours again. And that vow has haunted and taunted me throughout my career.

For now, though, this shift seemed my only option if I wanted to work in a television newsroom. That opportunity I was counting on? I didn't think it would find me in the wee hours of the morning in the ABC News bullpen, where I was surrounded by young hopefuls and folks who had been scrambling their way up the network news ladder for years. I looked around and realized there weren't a lot of role models for young women hoping to get on the air—and what few there were tended to work at the network level. I'd have to start my on-air career at the local level, of course, but the convention in local news back then was to hire a Ken-and-Barbie-type team to anchor the evening and late-night newscasts, and I came from a family where we dismissed the bubble-headed banter you heard between stories. It was a nightly ritual in our house when I was growing up to mock the malapropisms and the artless, witless, mindless insights that passed for commentary on our local channels. We Brzezinskis were a tough room, and as a result there wasn't a single person who stood out to me in the business as someone I wanted to emulate.

That said, there was a lot to admire about the role of a local reporter. Reporters are entrusted with the care and feeding of news and information to their neighbors, and a huge responsibility attaches to that trust. I thought about this a lot during those interminable late-night shifts. It was the best way to slog through the tedium and exhaustion—as I recall, I made a lot of copies and fetched a ton of coffee—to imagine where I might fit next on the broadcast news spectrum. Like every other would-be reporter, I knew full well that I'd have to start at the local level, so I set my mind to it. I loved the fact that people looked to television news for answers and insights. I loved the points of connection reporters could make with their subjects and with the whole community. And I absolutely hated that network overnight shift.

I lasted at ABC for about nine months—working the night shift and looking for a better job during the day. I finally found one at a small Fox station in Hartford, Connecticut. There'd be some drudge work there, too, I realized, but there'd also be daylight, in every sense of the term, so I counted this as my first big break. WTIC-TV, Channel 61, was still in the dark ages when I got there in 1990. We used typewriters and those big, clunky phones. I was twenty-two years old, and the world of television news was changing—but most of those changes had yet to reach Channel 61. This was just as well, because it kind of leveled the playing field for me.

Like me, the station was just starting out. Hartford was one of the top thirty television markets in the country in terms of households reached, and yet you'd never know it from the small-town vibe in our newsroom. Remember those old Andy Hardy movies, where Judy Garland, Mickey Rooney, and company all banded together to put on a show? Well, there was some of that *Hey! Let's put on a newscast!* enthusiasm among our group. There was a sense that we were all in this thing together, figuring it out as we went along.

I worked initially on the assignment desk, and I did my share of "beat checks." I can still tell you the phone numbers for the Hartford police, the Connecticut State Police, the Bristol, Manchester, Avon, and New London departments, and many, many more. I got to know many police chiefs and public information officers. At Channel 61, at last, I was able to think of myself as a working journalist. The station didn't even have a weekend newscast when I got there—truly a bare-bones operation. My job was to chase down stories, follow up on leads, and basically help our few reporters and producers figure out what was what before they went out into the field. I was learning the landscape, making key contacts, and keeping on the lookout for that next rung up the ladder.

I made many mistakes—but I took the position that each mistake offered a valuable learning experience. And for the most part, this was true, so I used those first few months on the job to learn the business in a trial-by-fire sort of way, and to take in what I could about local news in general and Hartford in particular. Our shared growing pains in our upstart newsroom eased soon enough, and it wasn't long before we were doing a good job, covering the city and the region, breaking our own stories and becoming a fixture on the local news scene.

There was something else going on in that newsroom. Something far more brilliant, far more personal. The best reporter at the station, Jim Hoffer, asked me to go running with him up a mountain. And so we did. We also climbed another mountain together: we ended up getting married. He knew that's where we were headed on our third date, when I told him that he should never call me again if he wasn't interested in the concept of getting married. I wasn't wasting time with anyone who didn't have the same plans. I could tell Jim had tremendous potential—as a journalist, no question; but more important, as a man. He was someone to climb all the mountains with.

Jim and I never told anyone we were dating, which helped me observe him from afar in the newsroom. I marveled at his talent as a reporter and a storyteller. I admired his integrity and honesty. He had come upon his gifts from far different circumstances in life. A child of the welfare system, he grew up in countless apartments with his three brothers and a mother who battled severe bipolar disorder all her life. Because of her illness and all the complications that came with it, Jim and his family moved every six months or so. He never really had a "home"— just an ever-changing set of challenging new environments. After high school, he left his small Pennsylvania town to go to college without even telling anyone, hitchhiking to Temple University and ultimately graduating with highest honors. Everything he ever did, he did himself, with no support or encouragement or parents convincing him that he was brilliant and talented, and that gave great texture to his reporting and writing.

I noticed that Jim had a way of connecting with all people, from the dirt poor to top political leaders. He was the same with everyone, because everyone was the same to him. He had a way of making them know that without ever having to say it. I watched raw tape of his interviews with little old ladies and murder victims in the projects, assessing the material that hadn't made the cut to see what kind of a man he was. Here's a little-known newsroom secret: raw tape is like a truth serum. What's left on the cutting room floor often holds the ugly stuff you don't want anyone to see—like how you ask someone if they'd be willing to talk, how you get them to look at you and not at the camera, how you treat the crew, all under the pressure of impossible deadlines. That's where an impatient, self-centered TV-type shows his or her true colors. I wanted to know whether Jim was husband material. He was that and much more. I had found the one. I was twenty-three, and it felt like I was behind schedule, but Jim was worth the wait! It was right there in all that raw tape.

As it happened, Jim's first big opportunity coincided with mine. The station had just added a weekend newscast, and Jim had been tapped to anchor. On his first Saturday night broadcast there was a double murder in the projects at the north end of Hartford. And here's where I came in: no one was available to cover it. So they sent me out. My big break! It was the middle of winter, impossibly cold, and I was wearing a short skirt and high heels. It never occurred to me I'd be on the air that night, or sent outside in those frigid temperatures. I looked and felt ridiculous. Indeed, I was ridiculous.

The name of the housing project where the homicides had taken place was Stowe Village. Folks spilled out of their apartments when they heard all the sirens and tried to muscle their way into our shot. People were throwing bottles at me while our cameras were rolling. They were screaming, "Bitch, get out of here!" and "Whore!" My outfit certainly didn't help. The killings didn't turn out to be racially motivated, but we didn't know that just yet, and there was a real racial hostility directed at me and my crew. I could *feel* the simmering rage and resentment in the air. These people were hopelessly poor, and pissed about it, and I might as well have been wearing a sandwich board stating, "I grew up in a rich, elite family! Please, beat me senseless!"

My photographer, Todd LaBrecht, seemed embarrassed to be with me, and I didn't blame him. He was constantly sighing and rolling his eyes. They weren't exactly cheering me on back in the newsroom, either. I could feel the tension there as well. I had a sense of being exposed, with no one to protect me. The reality was that I was still just a kid, the daughter of the former national security adviser, just a couple months into my first job, so there were many reasons not to like me. My future husband, on his first night at the anchor desk, was wishing me well, but he was likely alone in this. I wouldn't go so far as to say all my colleagues were rooting for me to fail, but quite a few were. That's the way this business works. It eats its young—especially its young women.

The Stowe Village double murder was shaping up as the lead that night, so there was a lot of pressure to get on the air and hit the ground running. I was petrified, unable to eat, and strung out with stress. In a perfect world, my first on-air report would have been a nothing-special visit to a panda at the zoo, or something similarly innocuous at the back of the broadcast, in that feel-good spot just after the weather, with people pulling for me in the newsroom. But this was a big, breaking story, with an unruly and offensive crowd shouting ugly, hateful things at me, and a group of "colleagues" at the station eager to watch me choke.

At the time, I thought I was doing a terrible job, but then I looked at the tape later that night and saw that it wasn't so bad. Not great, but totally acceptable. There was enough in my report to think I might land another assignment. I had a good presence. I'd asked the right questions, of the right people. I had the same basic information as every other reporter in town, so no one *beat* me on the story. But underneath all those basics, I could see I was nervous. I might have been good enough for this upstart station, for this one newscast, but I wasn't good enough to lift myself up and out and on to the next thing. I knew I'd have to find a way to absorb all sorts of distractions and focus on what I had to do when I was out on a story. I would learn from these struggles and figure out a way not to make the same mistakes again. I might make a whole set of new mistakes, but I'd figure it out before long.

Jim gave me his version of a compliment when I saw him later. He said I did "a nice job"—and that's really all it was. I'd covered the lead story without embarrassing myself or my station. I appreciated the honesty—an honesty we still offer each other when it comes to our work and our life.

I went out on the follow-up story the next day, and I managed to make a strong connection with a family member of one of the murder victims. It was, by every objective measure, a good second-day story. The weather was still impossibly cold, but this time I was dressed for it. I'd decided not to think about whatever resentment might be brewing toward me among my colleagues. I was a little less nervous. And this time, despite all those long hours, waiting in the cold for a comment from a police department spokesperson, I realized that I loved what I was doing. It was grueling and gritty, but I felt like I belonged no place else. That first night, less than twenty-four hours earlier, it felt like I'd made the biggest mistake of my young life, putting myself out there in such an unprepared, unfocused way, but now I found the feeling of belonging that I had been looking for. It was only day two of my on-air career, but already it was starting to feel like I had arrived.

I stayed on at WTIC-TV in Hartford for about a year. After that inauspicious first night at Stowe Village, I became one of the station's primary reporters—which wasn't saying a whole lot considering that we were a small Fox station in a market of entrenched network affiliates. Still, it was something, and I was determined to make the most of it. *Making the most of it*, by the way, didn't include making any kind of serious money. My first full-time salary at Channel 61 was $18,000, which meant that after rent and groceries there was basically nothing left.

In any case, it was a full-time job, and I was gradually becoming a real on-air fixture. Things were going well with Jim, too—so much so that before long we started to talk about a future together. I could see my career taking shape and my family, too. Jim wasn't so confident at first, given his childhood experiences, but we worked on this together, negotiating our hopes and dreams over bottles of wine after the Saturday night broadcasts. He was anchoring and occasionally filling in on the more prominent weeknight newscasts, and going out on more and better stories, while I was slotted into our regular rotation of general-assignment reporters. Things couldn't have been going any better for either one of us—or for the two of us as a couple.

As it happened, I was the first one to move on from Channel 61, but I didn't get very far. I took a job at the CBS affiliate in town—WFSB, Channel 3. It was an opportunity most of my colleagues would have rejected, because it was a step up only in terms of the scope and reach of the station itself. It was the same market, after all, so in this one respect it was almost a lateral move, and my new position was only a freelance gig, so in terms of my paycheck and my job security it was a clear step back.

But where others might have seen a downgrade, I saw an opportunity. It's been one of the great themes of my life and career, to take a step back in order to move forward, and for the first time I looked at my prospects in just this way. It was a simple equation, really. A big, powerhouse station like WFSB that reached clear across the state and through much of New England seemed to offer a far more promising outlook for an up-and-coming reporter than the Fox station where I'd gotten my start, even if it meant I'd essentially have to start all over again. Add to this the bonus of changing jobs without physically moving out of Hartford, and in this way allowing my relationship with Jim to continue on its course, which was extremely important to me. I knew I would have to work hard to get to that place where marriage could fit in alongside everything else.

I started having second thoughts as soon as I gave notice.

Gayle King was one of the main Channel 3 anchors, smack in the middle of an eighteen-year run as the face of the station. Up and down our roster of on-air reporters, there were rising stars and prominent personalities. It was like playing for the Red Sox instead of their Triple A minor-league farm team. Right away, I worried I might be in over my head. I worried they'd use me only a day or two here and there, and that I'd never be able to pay my rent. I worried I'd somehow get off to a slow start and never get a chance to show my new bosses what I could do. Mostly, I worried I'd left the *real* opportunity behind, at Channel 61. It was a time in my career when I needed to take this kind of risk, but at the same time the potential for failure ran high, so I was left with the agonizingly vague feeling that even though I had everything to gain, I also had quite a lot to lose.

This was around the time CBS News became a part of my identity, my ideal as a reporter. I'd always appreciated the mystique of CBS News. Remember, I came of age in a genuine television-news household. We *always* watched the nightly news—and the network news magazine shows as well. My father had been interviewed by pretty much everyone, and he liked to watch the shows that had him on, but he also had his set notions regarding the tone and style of each network—and CBS, owing mostly to *60 Minutes* and *Face the Nation* and Walter Cronkite and Dan Rather, stood apart. That respect for CBS was handed down to me, almost by osmosis, and now that I was a part of a network outpost, a sense of tradition seemed to really take hold of me. WFSB-TV Channel 3 was a well-respected affiliate, where folks carried the CBS banner with honor, and I began to feel the weight and might of the network-news division almost from the moment I signed on, even in this once-removed sort of way.

My very first assignment for Channel 3 was another big murder story—this time in a tough part of New Haven known as Newhallville. By this point, I'd started to feel somewhat comfortable as a reporter, but in truth I didn't really have my chops yet. That was all well and good when I'd been toiling in relative obscurity at the Fox station, but not so good now that I had put myself out in front. I was still a bit tentative on the air—and I knew this would now be glaringly apparent. And here's another thing: up in Hartford, I knew my way around, but down in New Haven I was flying blind. I knew nothing, no one. I felt again like my career was riding on this first assignment.

I had just turned twenty-four, and it was a lot of pressure to have on my shoulders on a single story, but I like to think I rose to the occasion. Check that: maybe *rose to the occasion* is overstating things a bit. Let's just say I didn't fall flat. Let's just say I didn't give the guy who sent me out on the story a reason to rethink his decision. Once again, it looked like this murder story was going to be the lead, but it was also shaping up as a "slam"—meaning the kind of developing, unfolding story that continues to develop and unfold right up until our broadcast. There was all this pressure to get tape back to the studio in time for us to "make page"—to avoid missing our slot and having to bump the story to later in the newscast.

We ended up hitting one glitch after another, and most of them had to do with my unfamiliarity with the city, the crew, and the way things worked at my new station. I nearly didn't make it on the air at all, but someone must have been watching over me that night, because we managed to get it done just in time, and it aired at the top of the broadcast. By every outward measure, the report went well. I kept my facts straight and my emotions in check. I interviewed all the right people and got all the necessary information. And we cobbled together all the right footage to help us put together a fine, polished piece.

As we wrapped for the night, I allowed myself a small sigh of satisfaction. I thought, *Okay, Mika. Looks like you'll live to see another day on the air.* Happily, I did, along with a few more after that. That's how you have to take it when you're working freelance—one day at a time. You keep trying to string together enough positive impressions to allow you to stick around for a while.

As it played out, I worked fairly steadily after that first report, and within a year I was promoted to full-time status—making up the ground I might have lost by leaving WTIC-TV. Somewhere in that first year, I told my bosses that Jim and I were getting married, which was not only good for us but good for our careers. Jim had moved to WTNH-TV, Channel 8, the ABC affiliate based in New Haven; our stations were now going head-to-head in the ratings, because even though the stations were based in different cities, we were competing in the same television market, so our relationship generated some local headlines. We made good copy—even more so when I became WFSB's Shoreline bureau chief, based in New Haven. We were direct competitors as well as husband and wife.

We moved into a tiny, ramshackle apartment above a garage in Branford, Connecticut. It was such a rinky-dink place—you could see the cars below through the floorboards in our living room—but it was on the beach, and it was very cute and romantic and simple. There was a single-burner stove in the kitchen. There were hardly any closets. We kept our clothes on racks in the middle of the room. We were both working so much, we were hardly there.

Jim and I had managed to climb that broadcast news ladder without really leaving town, so our personal life continued without interruption. He was promoted to investigative reporter at WTNH. There was a lot going on in New Haven, it turned out, so there was always something interesting to cover: murder, fires, graft, corruption . . . you name it, we had some version of it. Sometimes Jim and I would find each other while chasing stories. One afternoon, my photographer Andy Halpin heard something on the police scanner that sounded like a wild police chase. A car stolen. A woman screaming. He heard the words ". . . at the corner of Chapel Street and . . ." He realized that whatever was happening was just two blocks away, so he grabbed his clunky forty-eight-pound video camera and we started to run for it. When we got to the corner, near Claire's Deli, we were disappointed at first. We found some cops interviewing a woman. No big deal. We turned to leave, but before we could get very far the woman started to scream. She said, "Here it comes!" and "That's my car!" and "There he is!" Apparently, this woman's stolen car was speeding by just as she was being questioned by the police—with the thief at the wheel! An escapee from the local prison, no less. The cops took off after him. We took off after them. We hitched a ride with a woman driving a van and Andy shot video of this wild chase out the side door—all of it like something out of *Starsky and Hutch*—very exciting! The streets of New

Haven had turned into the Wild West. Sirens and lights every-where. Cops on horseback galloping through the streets. Andy was capturing all this great video for our exclusive story. That is, we'd *thought* we had an exclusive, until I saw Jim and his photographer Mark Laganqa running the same gauntlet. Now it felt like we were in the middle of a *Seinfeld* episode—and Jim was Newman!

Jim beat me that night with better writing and video. But I don't think I minded too terribly much. In fact, there was a moment when we were standing very nearly side by side, live at six o'clock, doing our separate stand-ups for our respective stations, and I thought, *This is totally cool.* Like some broad-cast-news version of Tracy and Hepburn, the two of us were battling it out at work and coming together at home. Two years later, I learned I was pregnant.

I'd been doing some fill-in work on the anchor desk, and unbeknownst to me, the station manager had me in mind to fill that role on a more regular basis on the morning broadcast. Here I was, prepared to take one of my trademark steps *back*, just as soon as I announced my condition, and management had me in mind for a very visible step *forward*.

Before I even had a chance to tell them, they offered me the job. I thought, *Now what do I do?* I was so excited about my pregnancy, but now I was dreading having to tell my boss. Too often, working women put themselves through these terribly anxious moments when it comes time to inform man-agement that they're having a baby, or getting married, or whatever, only to find out that management is incredibly supportive and accommodating. That's how it shook out for me at WFSB. I was terribly anxious—and then, wonderfully surprised.

The conversation between me and my news director Marc Effron went something like this:

MIKA: I am so, so sorry to spring this on you, Marc, but I'm pregnant. Jim and I are having a baby. I'm really hoping this doesn't cause any problems with my new job as morning anchor. Really, I'm so sorry. I know it's not what you had in mind.
MARC [*after a long pause that could have gone either way*]: Mika, that's terrific. That's so great for you. Really. And why are you sorry? This will be great for ratings!

In all the time spent fretting about how that conversation might go, it never went like that—but then I guess I wasn't thinking like a news director. It was as if I could see Marc Effron flipping through the pages of a calendar in his mind and trying to figure out if there was any way the baby could arrive during sweeps.

I started my new job as morning anchor the following Monday. Typically, morning newscasts at the local level air *before* the network morning shows, so this meant a 5 AM to 7 AM newscast each morning, a story shoot right after, with a healthy commute tacked on between New Haven and Hartford. If I'd been paying good and full attention, I would have seen the job for what it was—a return to the dreaded overnight shift, because I'd have to be up by about two each morning in order to dress, make the long drive to Hartford, and prepare for our sunrise newscast. Instead, I was so overjoyed that the station had these big plans for me, and that everybody was actually happy about my pregnancy, that I failed to consider the logistics of that morning anchor slot.

This time around, though, it didn't seem as bad—and I have to think it's because I had the rest of my life in order. The hours were still killer, the upside-down schedule still meant I was never on the same body clock as anyone else, but I was married to a great guy, with a baby on the way and a bright future on the air at a good-size CBS affiliate.

All of which now leads me to believe that when life is good and things are right you talk yourself into thinking you can get used to anything.

THREE

Up to the Minute

MARRIAGE AND WORK were aligned.

Of course, there were some challenges to keeping both moving along at full speed—and looking back I think I ignored most of them, perhaps on the theory that if I kept moving forward life would surely get easier. I contented myself with the fulfillment of a beautiful relationship, a baby on the way, and a job on the rise. Any career snags would have to announce themselves loudly, because I wasn't about to go looking for them.

I was deep into hard-charging, *say-yes-to-anything* mode. Moving forward, no matter what. If there were trouble spots or warning signs, at work or at home, I wouldn't see them. I wouldn't hear them. And I dared not give them voice. I was blessed with so many opportunities, I believed it was my due to take them all and make everyone proud. Even when it was too much to handle. That's what started to happen with my morning news gig: the commute slowly wore me down, and one day I looked up and realized life and work were not quite the paradise they seemed. The schedule took a lot out of me. I was pregnant, after all. I was human, after all. I wasn't meant to be keeping such ridiculous hours, for such an open-ended stretch. It wasn't natural, I started to think. A 2 AM wake-up call? In the beginning, there was the adrenaline rush and the excitement of a big new job, but the freshness fell away soon enough and my body started to feel the way it did when I'd worked the overnight shift at ABC as a desk assistant—constantly nauseous, nervous, exhausted, frayed, fried.

Not long after this slow-burning epiphany, Jim and I decided that the thing to do was quit our comfy, bungalow-type digs by the beach and move closer to the station. It was a desperation move—but it was the only move, really. You'll notice that I offer no suggestion here that I even considered stepping back from the morning news job; I just made the changes I could make in my personal life that might help me see it through. In this way, as in so many others, Jim and I were a *reactive* couple—as opposed to a *proactive* one. We'd typically wait for something to go wrong, or to not quite work out according to plan, before thinking about how to go at it a little differently, and then we'd try another strategy to get it right. Whatever it took.

Most of the people I know in television news approach their lives and careers in the same way. Our m.o. was to jump at opportunities as long as they seemed to make sense, which was how we'd landed at this latest decision to move closer to Hartford. It meant Jim would have a longer drive down to New Haven, but that seemed like a fair trade to save me some time in the morning. It also meant we'd have to give up the beach and the *Barefoot in the Park* charms of that ramshackle garage apartment—another fair trade, we both thought.

We ended up buying a house in West Hartford, which struck us both as a brilliantly perfect town. The house was perfect, too, in a storybook sort of way. Not too big, but room enough for the new baby and perhaps another down the road. It was just right. And best of all, my commute would now be seven minutes door-to-door! Really, it was the difference between waking up in the middle of the night and waking up (very, very) early in the morning—and at the time that difference was everything. I set it up in my head that these extra few minutes each morning would turn my impossible schedule into a manageable one, and in this way the matter was settled.

For the time being, anyway.

That house, that setting . . . it was like something out of my girlhood fantasies. It's how I'd always pictured my life, when I stopped to fast-forward my hopes and dreams and fully imagine my future. I'd always wanted to have that full picture of husband, family, career. And it really was a *full* picture. As much as I wanted to work in television, it wasn't just about the job for me. It wasn't even mostly about the job. There were all these component parts, and the idea was to fit them together in a coherent, fulfilling way. The job was an important piece, but I was after the whole beautiful puzzle.

You'd think this would be the default approach for women in the workplace, but that's far from the case. I don't understand the career-first approach, but I encounter it all the time. A lot of women I know start out thinking, *Work, work, work.* It's only later, when they feel they have some job security and some bankable, marketable experience that they allow themselves to think about a family. At that point, the mantra becomes *Husband, husband, husband.* Or, after that, *Kids, kids, kids.* But that wasn't me. All along, I was hoping to meet a guy when we were young enough to go through these motions together. I wanted our careers to be a part of our shared journey. I wanted us to grow into what we would become . . . together. That's what my parents had accomplished—challenging each other and being challenged. Up and down, together. From time to time, maybe one of our careers would have to simmer on the back burner, depending on what was going on with the other one's career, or with our family, but the test would be to grow together as partners, parents, and individuals. And I wanted to have children while I could still enjoy them. I wanted to crawl around on the floor with them, and play in the sandbox, and take in their world from their level.

For the life of me, I can't understand why so many women wait until the age of thirty to even think about children. And that's just the *start* of the conversation for them. The risks associated with pregnancy increase as each year goes by, and it's unbelievable to me that anyone would deliberately choose to put off having children until they're deeper and deeper into that risk zone. If it doesn't work out that you're in a position to start a family until later on in life, that's one thing. But if you're actually "putting off" the call of children for some vague or far-off opportunity at work, that's another thing entirely. Our bodies perform best when we're young; our chances of having a successful pregnancy and a healthy baby are greater when we're younger. So why not play into that?

Everywhere I look, I see women putting their careers above all else. They put off living, and at the other end, when their careers fall out from under them, their lives are suddenly empty. There's nothing to fill the space where the work had been. For me, when it was my turn to get fired—and, sooner or later, it's *everyone's* turn—I had a whole other world waiting for me. I had two beautiful daughters, and a loving husband, and a whole constellation of other interests and activities and places to funnel my energy. Make no mistake, I missed my work terribly. But I never once felt like my career had robbed me of any of these other elements in my life. Whenever I talk to young women about their lives and careers, I make it a special point to remind them to look for a good partner as fervently as they might seek out professional opportunity. Not in a desperate, personal-ad sort of way—but just by staying open to whatever comes along. Usually, at the end of my spiel, my audience looks at me from behind a few shades of disbelief, as if it's the first time they've ever heard a career woman speak to them so bluntly about placing an emphasis *away* from career. But I insist. Marriage, career, children. Career, marriage, children. However you bundle it, I tell them, make it all happen. If that's what you want, then go ahead and reach for it and give it time to happen.

Jim and I decided early on that our family would be our foundation. Whatever opportunities happened for us at work would be absorbed into whatever opportunities were happening for us at home. And yet this piece of my personal puzzle took such a long time falling into place that I'd started to worry. I shouldn't have, but I did. I was twenty-six when I got married, and that felt very old to me at the time. I was twenty-eight when I got pregnant, and that, too, seemed a little behind schedule. I always wanted to have my children while I was young, and get my career going alongside my children so we could experience everything together. And I just don't understand why women wait until they're thirty or thirty-five to even consider getting pregnant. Real fulfillment comes from taking on challenge, and embracing it, not putting it off. And having children at twenty-three would have been amazing, but it didn't work out that way. I wanted it all, together, and I was looking for marriage and career with equal fervor, but I just couldn't find the right guy. For the longest time. And when I found him I wanted to get right to work, because he was so amazing and I wanted to have his children.

Indeed, the moment I knew wholeheartedly that Jim was for me came about six months into our relationship when he took me to his hometown in Pennyslvania to meet his family. His mother was living in a shack of an apartment. It wasn't Jim's childhood home—not by a long stretch. His mother struggled with a severe bipolar disorder, and had been in and out of treatment for decades. She'd also been in and out of so many apartments and homes that Jim had long ago stopped counting. Her disorder had left her so unstable that she moved every six months, usually selling off her furniture and all of her worldly possessions with each transition. It struck me as such an uncertain, untethered way to live.

Jim had explained all this to me, early on in our relationship, but it took meeting his mother and seeing her suffering firsthand for me to understand what Jim's life must have been like growing up—and, what it was like for him still, picking up the pieces for his mother. We walked up a dark staircase in the small building where she was living at the time, and opened the door to his mother's apartment. The first thing I noticed was that the door couldn't fully open because Jim's mother had placed the cat litter box directly behind it, so we had to kind of slither our way inside. Then we had to walk along this dark, narrow hall, and it felt like that scene in *The Wizard of Oz* where Dorothy is walking through the haunted forest and the trees keep grabbing at her from all sides. There was so much crap hanging on the walls; it felt like it was tugging at me as I passed. Then we all sat down in dusty chairs, in a room that was so filled with clutter you couldn't step directly on the floor if you tried. It was hard to imagine that a person could accumulate so much mess and disorder in just a few months, but there it was.

Once we were all seated, Jim's mother started going on and on about some problem with her ex-husband's wife, and Jim listened patiently and lovingly for about twenty minutes, trying to calm her down. As I watched this scene, I could see that the picture Jim had painted about his difficult background was dead-on accurate. If anything, he'd soft-pedaled his circumstances, probably because he didn't want to scare me away. But the way he was with his mother was a revelation. It was just like he was with the old lady at the Durham fair, with the governor of Connecticut, or with me: fair. *Really* fair. And he took his mother seriously. He listened to her. He cared. He loved his mother, and I came to love her, too—and to value what she offered to the world, and the gift she had created in Jim.

It turned out to be the perfect time to be pregnant as far as my career was concerned, because it ended up coinciding with my move to that morning anchor seat. And it worked out just fine in terms of my biological clock, too. I was still going out on stories, still chasing after murderers with my growing belly. I was in great shape. I jogged five miles every day, right up until I gave birth. I ate right. The only thing I didn't do by the book was sleep.

The happy surprise for me at work was that being pregnant made me a better reporter. I gained a deeper appreciation for the emotional elements of each story. It also made me more relatable to viewers—a key factor for a local news anchor. Local news viewers love it, I was told. Pregnant news anchors mean big ratings, I learned. That in itself was no major revelation; it's been transparent since women started working in front of the cameras. But what was news to me was the way my pregnancy changed my approach to the job; it opened me up to a new way of looking at the world. As a wife and mother-to-be, I could approach each story with a full-on perspective.

Now that my own complete picture was coming into focus for me, I took the time to appreciate it. Every day, I marveled at it. I had to pinch myself each time I walked through the kitchen door of our adorable house. It was so bright, so simple . . . so *validating*. I was making $40,000 a year, which was not great money for an anchor job in 1995, but it was enough. I was married to a terrific guy, feeling wonderful. He was making a sound salary, too. We had everything to be thankful for, everything to look forward to.

We documented my entire pregnancy—on the air, live, every morning—which is how it goes in local news. We had two hours of airtime to fill, so there was ample opportunity for my co-anchor, Brendan Keefe, to make comedic comments about my big belly. I became addicted to peanut butter and ate two big toasted bagels slathered with Jif every morning on the set. I wore adorable maternity clothes. We played the whole thing up, in every appropriate way, and the Connecticut viewers really loved it. They sent me gifts. They tuned in, in big numbers. Some even called in with heartfelt concern after I filed a late summer report on jet-ski safety. There I was, six months pregnant and riding the waves on Long Island Sound like some *Baywatch* biker chick. The viewers worried over me like I was family—and I suppose in a way I was.

Emilie finally came along in January 1996, and right away she filled all the spaces I didn't know we had. We named her for my grandmother and my mother, which I thought was fitting. My grandmother and mother had both helped to give me shape when I was a little girl, and now Emilie would give me shape as a young mother. It was all tied in, all of a piece, all at once.

As it happened, Emilie made her television debut the night she was born. Over the years, I've come to regard the integrating of my kids with my work as unnecessary, frivolous, and possibly even unhealthy, but at that time I was too distracted by the joys of new motherhood to give it serious thought. My pregnancy had been such an ongoing story—not only at my station, but at Jim's as well. It was a joint enterprise, so when Emilie was delivered at about nine o'clock in the evening, without a hitch, our thoughts turned immediately to the eleven o'clock newscast. Both stations had been calling for updates, and there were cameras waiting outside the delivery room. That's how we were conditioned to think, as local-news types: *How soon can we get this on the air?*

So what did I do? I cleaned myself up, put on some makeup and a sweet little white nightgown, and got ready for my close-up. Two hours later, our precious little Emilie was on the late news—on Channel 3 *and* Channel 8. I still remember the lead line: "It's not often that Channel 3 and Channel 8 can collaborate on a story, but . . ." Then we cut to cute me and my cute baby. So cute it was gross. But the viewers ate it up.

All during my pregnancy, I continued to make inroads at the station. They used me more and more. After the baby was born, I was determined not to miss a beat. Emilie sat in my arms on my first day back. I started anchoring the noon newscast as well, and filling in for Gayle King at night, and basically working my butt off—but it didn't feel like work, because I loved what I was doing and I loved how things were with our family. I loved that the viewers were continuing to respond to me in my ever-changing role, and that I was able to handle whatever my bosses could throw at me.

We settled into a doable routine. I pushed through the early wake-up call, because it gave me some cherished quiet time with Emilie in the afternoons. And it balanced out against

Jim's schedule. We were making it work. I was breast-feeding at the time, and I couldn't get used to the public aspects of such a private matter. I was very embarrassed about it, so I spent a lot of time ducking behind the local grocery store—by the loading dock!—to avoid the uneasy stares of passersby. I got my running in each afternoon, pushing Emilie in her baby jogger. I had time to walk into town with my baby girl, pushing her stroller and looking like all the other young moms. I could even sneak in a nap during the day, when Emilie went down for her nap. Everything fit. Soon, there was talk at the station of making me the main anchor. And I found the time to get more involved in the community. I started doing work for local charities, such as Race for the Cure. I was feeling totally enriched and engaged as a wife, as a mother, as a journalist . . . as a woman.

It was all so perfect, in fact, that I'd catch myself thinking, *It just doesn't get any better than this.* Really, I could have seen myself anchoring the local news and living in our picture-perfect house forever, and it was during these same moments that I'd realize this stage in our lives couldn't last forever. I'd muse aloud to Jim, saying, "One of us is going to get a big network job and everything will come tumbling down." It wasn't a defeatist attitude, or a pessimistic view. Just a sense that no young family deserved such riches. I'd say, "This is just too perfect, too great, too much."

He couldn't help but agree.

* * *

For all my talk about embracing life in the fullest sense, and trying to keep my personal and professional priorities in balance, I was as guilty as every broadcast journalist I knew of wanting to "go network"—to land a job at ABC, NBC, or CBS on one of their national broadcasts. Maybe *guilty* is not the best word in this context. It's probably better to say that I was *vulnerable* to the siren call of CBS News. It had been drilled into me for so long that when you get the call from the network, you run to the phone. Like when the White House called for my father. You simply go, and the rest of the family falls in line.

I wasn't looking for a network job, but one came looking for me. A job anchoring the network's *Up to the Minute* overnight newscast—another graveyard shift gig, only this time I'd be sitting in a network anchor chair, and it would have my name on it.

For a beat or two in there, that's *all* I could think about.

The job wasn't mine just yet. I had to go down to New York and audition and meet with the CBS News management. I had to get my head around the fact that for some strange reason this was slotted as a freelance job, with no benefits, although the hours figured to add up to more than three times what I was making in Hartford—to about $150,000, which unfortunately wouldn't go very far if we were now going to be looking to move into the New York City housing market. I wasn't too worried about the benefits, because Jim was covered at Channel 8, but there was something tentative and tenuous in signing on for another day-rate job after I had been on such sure and solid footing in Hartford.

And yet despite all these question marks and potential negatives, I jumped at the job when it was finally offered to me—on May 2, 1997, my thirtieth birthday. A network job. *Not a bad birthday gift,* I thought at the time, but looking back I consider my decision to take this *Up to the Minute* job as the first in a series of misguided notions I would allow to shade my network news career—and the next ten years of my personal life as well. I was so overcome by the thought of working as a network newsperson that I put aside a fear in my gut that the schedule would be too much, given that working as a morning anchor in Hartford was already starting to be a challenge for this particular new mother. I chose instead to focus on the opportunity the job would provide me and our growing family. I looked at the recent "graduates" from the same anchor chair: Russ Mitchell, Sharyl Attkisson . . . Both were successful network newscasters whom I hoped to emulate. And Sharyl had had a baby on that shift, so I got to thinking that if she could make it work, then I could find a way to make it work as well.

Very quickly, I bought into the whole CBS News culture in such a way that nothing seemed more important than this one opportunity. That network anchor seat was such a powerful lure I never gave the horrible hours a truly focused thought. I hardly blinked at the freelance aspect of the job—although I certainly should have, because if it was such a great opportunity it would have come with a full-time salary and a pension and health benefits. I did worry that the schedule would pull me from Emilie and Jim and the world we were building, but we felt we could handle it. We had come this far. Jim had no such worries, because he'd come to this stage in his life from an entirely different place. To him, marriage was a complete blank slate, and a complete partnership. There were no preconceived roles. Either things would work out for us on this new schedule, or we'd make whatever adjustments we needed to get it right and keep moving.

So I jumped at the chance, with Jim's full support, and while I can't go so far as to say I regretted it right away, I'll say this: I regretted it soon enough. I allowed the job to define me in the worst possible ways. For one thing, the hours weren't just horrible. They were impossible. It was set up so that I had to pretape half of our newscast at nine o'clock each evening, because that's when we could get people to come in to the studio for our interview segments. The balance of the show was done live, with more of a skeleton crew, from two o'clock in the morning until five o'clock in the morning. Basically, it was a nine-to-five job—only it was the *wrong* nine-to-five. It was a grueling, killer schedule, and the absolute worst parts were those trapped hours between the nine o'clock taping and the live broadcast at two in the morning.

We put our West Hartford house on the market soon after I moved to CBS News, and we started looking for a place closer to New York. The loose plan was for Jim to commute to New Haven, which in theory wouldn't have been so terrible since he'd usually be going against rush-hour traffic in and out of New York, and because investigative reporters keep such odd, ridiculous hours anyway. I was by now constantly and relentlessly tired; I could barely process the changes to our routines. I was making bad decisions, thinking more about what would work for Jim's commute than for mine. I was thinking for everyone at once, trying to fill every hole in our new upside-down lifestyle, and feeling guilty that it was my job putting such a strain on our family.

Stupidly, we landed in Norwalk, Connecticut, about as close to Manhattan as we thought we could afford, even with my stepped-up day rate. For a while we had looked at houses in Westchester County, just north of the city, but we couldn't touch anything in a decent neighborhood, so Norwalk seemed like a good compromise. It really wasn't. Nothing against Norwalk, but it put me about an hour from the CBS News studios on West 57th Street in midtown Manhattan. It meant we'd need virtually full-time babysitting help in order to cover our two all-over-the-place schedules. It meant we would be totally in over our heads—all in the mad rush for me to pursue this impractical job I probably shouldn't have even considered in the first place.

Later on, going over this frantic period in my life, trying to understand my impulse and motivation, I began to realize that women sometimes make life-altering career decisions with a kind of gun to their heads. We put ourselves in these false do-or-die scenarios that leave us thinking if we don't overextend ourselves, or push, push, push after opportunities when they appear, that we'll never accomplish our goals or rise in the estimation of our peers. That was me, there on the CBS night shift, only I failed to consider that I'd already accomplished my primary goals: I was married to an amazing man, with a beautiful baby girl and a career I loved.

In my defense, I was helped along in this delusion. The

mere mention of the job so impressed my peers, my family, and my casual acquaintances that they reinforced for me that this was a great opportunity, one I dared not set aside. I started to look at the job as a kind of game-changer, in part because friends and colleagues saw it that way. Even Jim thought I had to go for it. For the record, and to their great credit, my parents were extremely worried about the schedule. They knew what riches I already had in hand—and how precious they were to me. But they also knew I was conditioned to strive toward the next goal—and for a broadcast journalist that meant taking whatever scraps the network might throw my way. And make no mistake, these were scraps.

This attitude is another one of the fundamental flaws in the way women approach their careers. The idea that I was only entitled to scraps is a long-standing and very female standard—one that would take me twenty years to get past. I never really stopped to think about what this network job might look like once I tried it on—and once I did, I couldn't admit to myself that it didn't fit. Really, it was all wrong, but by this point Jim and I felt we were too deep into this next phase of our lives to double-back and set things right. We were in a kind of shared denial, and as a result that first year at CBS News was a blur. I don't remember much about work. I don't remember much about being at home with Emilie. I don't remember much at all. Mostly, what resonates is the time I spent shuttling back and forth between work and home—in each direction fretting that it was taking me so damn long to get there. It felt to me like I was never precisely where I wanted to be. I took the train, mostly. Sometimes I drove, but parking was expensive and traffic was unpredictable. *Everything* was so expensive and unpredictable. The babysitter's hours. The house. That extra money was gone before it had a chance to accumulate any interest. And, in a palpable way, I could *feel* all that money and all that time and all that energy being drained from our accounts. Every day that went by, I was more exhausted, and there was never a moment to catch up, and there was never really anything to show for all the effort.

All at once, *all things at once* didn't seem like such a great idea.

If I had it to do all over again, I would not take that *Up to the Minute* job. When things go well during a certain time in your life, you can always look back and picture how things were; you remember how you felt, what you thought. But when things get a little out of control, you'll look back and wonder what the hell you were doing during that period, and that's what I'm left with here. I have no clear sense of our life in Norwalk, of my time with Emilie, of the factors that went into our decision to grow our family and have a second child, of Jim's pursuit of a job at WABC-TV, Channel 7 in New York. It was all just one mad scramble—and at the other end of it, I realize now, I made a great many mistakes. Most of these had to do with the fact that I was young and foolish and didn't take the time to calibrate my priorities with a sense of self and confidence. There was no strategy. Getting pregnant again while working that impossible schedule and raising a toddler wasn't a mistake, but maybe I should have considered what our lives might look like with two infants at home, with me commuting over an hour to my crummy overnight job in Manhattan, with Jim chasing down a new, bigger job in Manhattan, with me taking on more and more when I couldn't even handle what I already had.

We were very much on autopilot, and that's fine and necessary for certain stretches, but that was the norm for us, to run around like crazy and try to cram as much as we could into every moment. That kind of constant, full-tilt, all-out approach can only lead to some kind of collapse. By the time Carlie arrived, in June 1998, I was a little over a year into this frantic new schedule, Jim was signing on at WABC, and our heads weren't exactly in sync with our hearts.

Physically, I felt fine. The pregnancy had been another breeze, even on the night shift. I was out jogging again the day Carlie was born. But emotionally, I was spent. It was all we could do to make it to work each day and try to do a reasonably good job of things, then race home and relieve the babysitter and hope to do a reasonably good job of things there. That's all. We'd get through one day without a hitch and start in to worrying about the next. We were like air-traffic controllers, trying to keep everything on course, everything on schedule, everything up in the air so nothing would crash down around us.

I worked right up until Carlie arrived. During my last week on the air, a series of breaking news stories had me doing CBS News "Special Reports" all night long, interrupting our regular programming, so there was all the additional stress of being seen by management during prime time and being hugely pregnant. During one of the breaking news reports, I started feeling what I knew were labor pains, and called the doctor from my desk and told him I couldn't really peel away from what I was doing to get myself to the hospital. The pains were timing out at about an hour apart, so the doctor was not alarmed. He recommended taking a couple of sips of wine, which seemed to help. After that I started carrying wine in my purse in case there was breaking news.

When people looked up from their own crazy-hectic schedules and noticed mine, most seemed to gush over how exceptional it was for me to be pregnant, exercising, working at the network, taking care of Emilie. Not everyone, though. Again, for the record, my parents continued to voice their concerns to my deaf ears. I heard them and dismissed them, as if they were drug addicts telling me to just say no. I knew full well that they'd accepted great challenges throughout their marriage. They'd traveled the world and taken on two world-class careers and a tremendous amount of stress. For them, it all worked out. Life and work and marriage and family . . . all a grand success. They had a great relationship, and three grown, well-educated, worldly kids. I thought, *Who are they to tell me to slow down?*

Carlie's arrival was emblematic. Jim was off at an investigative-reporting conference in New Orleans. He was about to start his big new job, and he wanted to hit the ground running, so it made sense for him to go—except for the fact that I was due. In all fairness to Jim, I was the one who'd urged him to attend the conference, convinced that it would make him feel more confident as he started at WABC—and that this was the stance I needed to take as a supportive wife. Jim resisted, like any good husband and expectant father would have done, but I made a loud and compelling argument—so off he went, both of us hoping against hope that Carlie would not arrive early.

My mother came to stay with me, to help out with Emilie. I thought I had everything covered. Then, one evening into Jim's trip . . . my water broke. My loose backup plan was set in motion. Before Jim left, I'd reached out to a woman I didn't know very well and cast her in a key role. Her name was Diane Smith, and she'd worked with Jim at Channel 8. I liked her and she liked Jim, which meant she was a good judge of character. Plus, she lived relatively close—an important consideration, to be sure. I had called her and put it to her straight.

That phone call had the makings for one of the Top Ten Awkward Conversations of All Time, but Diane had such an open heart and an open mind that it actually went okay. At least it seemed to go okay from my end.

"Hi, Diane," I said when she picked up the phone. "It's Mika Brzezinski, Jim's wife. How are you?"

"I'm great, Mika," she said. "How are you feeling?"

I thought, *Okay, that's one notch in the plus column.* At least she remembered I was pregnant.

"Pretty good," I said. "Thanks for asking." Then I fumbled for a bit before continuing: "Ummm . . . Diane . . . I'm wondering if I could ask you a favor?"

"Sure," she said. "What's up?"

"Jim's going out of town next week," I explained, "to an

investigative reporter's conference. And I'm kind of supposed to have the baby. Ummm . . if that happens, and I'm hoping it won't and Jim will be back and everything will be fine, but if the baby comes . . . ummm . . . do you think you could take me to the hospital?"

I could actually hear the wheels spinning in Diane's head through the phone. I imagined the look on her face, which was probably crinkled up in *What-the-???* astonishment. Now it was Diane's turn to fumble. I think she laughed. "Ummm . . . sure, Mika," she finally said. "Anything for Jim." Then she marveled at how I was so selflessly sending Jim off to his investigative reporter's conference, and we tried to turn the conversation to more mundane matters—each of us probably hoping we'd never have to put our uncomfortable transaction into play.

At this point, I thought I'd do well to hang up before Diane had a chance to change her mind. I knew I was riding on the coattails of my universally loved husband for this favor. And I knew it was a favor I could never repay in kind. Who else would even *ask* for such a favor?

Diane took her commitment seriously. She approached her role like a good journalist. She realized that I didn't just need her to drive me to the hospital if Jim was out of town when the baby arrived. I'd need her to do a little bit more besides, so she and her husband Tom started reading baby books to prepare. She knew somehow this would fall on her watch. And it did.

I called her as soon as my water broke, and she and Tom jumped out of their beds and fumbled for their car keys and raced over to pick me up. I remember standing outside my house, waiting for them on the street. It was late at night, my mother was asleep with Emilie and I was in labor, thinking this wasn't exactly how I'd pictured my delivery—reaching out to a woman who was little more than an acquaintance, praying she would see me through.

While I was waiting, a gold-hubcapped car full of guys playing ridiculously loud rap music pulled up at the curb in front of me. They looked me up and down and sped off. I guess I made an odd picture, standing on the street like that, pregnant, waiting for a ride. Mercifully, that ride came soon enough.

Diane and I might have only been casual friends going in, but nothing bonds two women like going through childbirth together. We stayed up all night, laughing at the crazy business we were in and the people we knew in common. From time to time, we'd put a pin in our hysterics for me to take my labor breaths or power through a difficult contraction, but then we'd be right back at it. Then, about sixteen hours later, sort of as a capper, I had a baby. Two pushes and there was Carlie.

With Carlie, the name was a bit of an afterthought. We'd been working so hard, and dealing with our hectic, crazy, stressful lives that we just never got around to thinking about a name. We actually checked out of the hospital after she was born and realized as we were filling out the last of the paperwork that we didn't have a name. We scrambled to come up with ... *something*. We thought first of Lynn as a middle name, after Jim's best friend from growing up, a real constant in his turbulent life. And then Jim suggested the name Carly. He said, "I always liked that name."

I said, "You like Carly Simon, don't you?"

And he said, "Yeah, I guess that's where I got it."

So I agreed, but we spelled it with an *ie*, to match Emilie's name.

As long as I'm on it, Emilie's name hadn't come all that easily, either. Back in 1996, we were all organized, all over it. We had her name picked out as soon as we knew we were having a girl: Emilie, after my mother and grandmother. Only we were going to pronounce it "Emily," the way my grandmother pronounced it. My mother pronounced her name like Amelia Earhart, even though it was spelled the same way as her mother's. It's one of those names you can pronounce however you like, and here we'd decided we would pronounce it "Emily." That is, until four months after she was born, when I was driving Emilie to Pennsylvania to visit Jim's family and it was just the two of us in the car, and I could see her little face in the backseat in the rearview mirror. Her little cheeks, her little face, everything about her expression just seemed to scream *Emil-i-a*. She just didn't look like an Emily. So I changed it. For four months she had been "Emily," and now she was Emilie. Spelled the same way.

To this day, Diane's one of my closest friends, and I'll be forever grateful that she was there for me that night—a night, as I look back, that seems to symbolize how all over the place Jim and I were in our thinking. But also the beginning of a lasting friendship.

With Carlie now in the picture, there was nothing to do but continue to plow forward. *Is the baby healthy?* Check. *Am I healthy?* Check. *Are Emilie's needs being addressed?* Check, check, check. *What about a name? Carlie?* Check. Move on.

So that's just what we did. Literally. Two weeks later, in one hundred degree heat, I packed up our house and family and moved our worldly possessions from Norwalk into a big, run-down Victorian in Yonkers, New York, where my commute would be much easier. It reminded me of that great old house in *It's a Wonderful Life*, the one in the center of town that Donna Reed and Jimmy Stewart buy and turn into the centerpiece of their lives. My idea was we would fix it up and it would be the house of our dreams—another wacky notion. Who had time to fix up an old house? Here again I was pretty much on my own. My mom came back up from Virginia to help me unpack, but Jim was just starting out in his new job and staying in the city while he got acclimated, and neither one of us felt he could take the time away for a personal matter, so I slogged through the move with a newborn on my breast and a toddler at my feet. All these years later, I have this image in my head of little, fabulous Car-lie, resting in the front yard in a car seat that doubled as a kind of rocker, while I was perched on a jittery ladder, cutting branches from a cluster of giant trees in our yard that had been scraping the side of the house, as Emilie ran around not doing such a good job of keeping out of my way—all in 96 degree heat.

It was such an absurd scene! I was trying to be like my mother, I realized, blazing that trail through our back acres with her bare hands just after we moved to Virginia, but it felt like too much all at once. That I was out there at all, trimming brush and pulling ivy on the back of such a big move, two weeks after giving birth, with my two baby daughters underfoot . . . it's like I was some bionic pioneer woman when, really, a lot of these chores could have waited. I pulled a massive amount of ivy, too, as I recall—until blisters erupted on both hands. But I wanted our new house to look nice. I wanted our picture-perfect life to come quickly back into focus.

Regrettably, *waiting* wasn't exactly in my vocabulary, especially when it came to work—in part because it wasn't part of the CBS News ethos, either. Almost as soon as I got Carlie home from the hospital, I started thinking about returning to the overnight anchor chair. There's no reason I should have been thinking about work so soon after having a baby, but there I was. I was determined to make such a positive impression on my bosses at CBS that they would keep me in mind for any other opportunities that might open up in the news division. Mostly, though, I wanted them to just keep me in mind, period. For *anything* that might come next—especially opportunities that might get me off the night shift. This was a freelance position, after all, and even though I'd been there a full year I worried maternity leave would be an out-of-sight, out-of-mind scenario. If they managed to fill that *Up to the Minute* anchor seat with a suitable replacement, there'd be no incentive for them to take me back. Plus, the money was a real issue for us. I wasn't getting paid while I was out on leave, and we'd just bought this big old house, and there were all kinds of expenses to consider with the new baby. It felt as if there was a clock on my time away from the newsroom, and it kept ticking louder and louder.

And so, for all these reasons taken together, there was a lot of pressure to get back to work as quickly as possible. Pressure I put on myself, but also pressure from the station. Jim tried to distract me from all those pressures, but he wasn't doing such a good job of it. I started hearing from my co-anchor and my producers that they were having a tough time filling my spot. It was hit-or-miss with the anchors they were bringing in during my absence. I felt like I was deserting my post—even though the real reason they couldn't find a more permanent, more workable replacement was because no CBS correspondent would sign on for such a terrible schedule for anything more than a day or two, here and there.

I went back after only five weeks, long before I was ready. Before my household was ready. Before Carlie was ready. I was bone-tired, and my emotions were raw, and my circumstances still so brand-new. I wasn't myself. I don't think it was postpartum depression, because I wasn't really down about anything, but if I had to put a label on it I'd call it postpartum anxiety. That sounds about right. I cried a lot, as I recall. God knows what I was crying about, but I was so frazzled there was always a new batch of tears ready to start flowing, for some reason or other. I was on such a knife edge, anything could set me off. Or nothing at all. Once, I sat down on the bathroom floor at CBS and started weeping. At just that moment, Karen Sacks, the executive producer of *Up to the Minute*, happened to walk in. She took one look at me and got right down on the floor and commiserated with me. As a mother herself, she knew what I was going through. I hadn't meant for anyone at work to see me so distraught and off my game, but Karen was great about it. In fact, everyone at *Up to the Minute* was great about it, I think because they all knew what I was giving up to be there. We were a small, tight group, and in my short time there I'd never played the anchor-diva card. I was hardworking and honest and approachable, a real team player. That's how I always wanted these good people to see me. Now especially.

And yet for all my foolish pride and brio it never occurred to me that in selling this image of myself as a tough, resilient journalist and reliable teammate I was selling myself short— and setting myself and my family up for a big fall.

FOUR

Falling

I'D HAD MY SECOND CHILD and moved our family into a big old house in five weeks. As my return to work approached on the calendar, I'd started to feel down about it. My body language was *off*. I'd actually walk past a mirror and catch a glimpse of myself, already looking weary. My entire demeanor seemed to sag, as if just the prospect of that looming grind was too much for me to carry.

A month back into that grind, it wasn't working. The weight was too much. I was so completely strung out I couldn't even remember what the job had looked like before Carlie was born. I was trying to balance the tough hours with the needs of two babies and a marriage. I wanted to be available and "fun" for my husband, for my babies, for my friends and colleagues. Instead, I was crying all the time. We were still living out of boxes at home, and the fixer-upper improvements we'd imagined for our new house seemed further and further from ever getting under way. Already, the house was turning out to be a leaky, moldy nightmare.

On the work front, I was starting to realize I'd made a huge mistake in racing back. Plus, I looked like hell—not a good look when you work in a visual medium. This was the overnight broadcast, produced on the cheap; there were no hair or makeup people on staff to help me cover up the stress and strain. I had to do my own, and when you're running on empty like I was during this period, it's tough to give something so mundane and simple the attention it truly deserves. And yet in television the way you look is such a huge part of the job. It matters. You might think it shouldn't, but it does. When I first signed on at CBS the year before, I'd managed to look pretty good. For most of that time, I was pregnant and glowing, so the camera picked up on all that radiant happiness and joy, which certainly helped. Now, though, I felt absolutely horrible—as well as horribly conflicted—and the camera picked up on that, too.

My body wasn't ready to climb back on that unyielding overnight treadmill, and neither was my soul. I just couldn't get my head around the fact that I was being pulled from my two beautiful daughters at such a critical time. A time we'd never get back. I went through the motions at work, but my mind and spirit were at home.

I had rushed back because I worried I would let my bosses down if I didn't. But I was also worried I would crack my super-working-mother-and-wife image. I really and truly wanted to please the people most important to me. I wanted my husband to have everything he needed. I wanted us to have time together and money to pay the bills. I wanted my children to grow up and be proud of their mother and see all the possibilities that were available to them in the world. I wanted my colleagues and bosses to see how committed I was to the work they were giving me.

I wanted to be able to do it all, but it was all just out of reach. On the home front, I wasn't sleeping at all. It wasn't just my ridiculous schedule keeping me from getting my rest. It was being unable to set my mind at ease. It was struggling to find quality, focused time to be with Carlie and her big sister, Emilie, when I was home, and adjusting my body clock to the new rhythms all around. I was breast-feeding—this added to my exhaustion. I was walking around withered and exhausted and barely able to feed Carlie because I was so tired. Whenever I tried to pump or to nurse, it felt like it was literally sucking the life out of me. I didn't feel like Carlie was thriving, or getting anything out of me because I had nothing to give, so after about four or five weeks I put her on formula. Whenever I did get a chance to lie down, I'd usually stare at the walls and wonder why I couldn't sleep. I would hear my babies crying and feel like I should get up and be with them—and once that thought entered my racing head there was no shaking it.

Looking back, I can't believe I was even able to navigate those overnight newscasts and then find my way back to our leaky, moldy fixer-upper. I was operating on fumes and muscle memory, just. At the end of every shift, I couldn't get out of that newsroom fast enough, I was so desperate to get home. The Friday commutes had some extra-special urgency to them because I had the entire weekend ahead of me. They represented a reprieve of a kind. And the promise of a full night's sleep—a cherished luxury. I'd have my girls and Jim to care for, and I couldn't wait to get started on it. As soon as we rolled the credits on *Up to the Minute* and threw to *CBS News This Morning*, I willed myself home. At times, I was asked to fill in on what is now called *The Early Show*, between 7AM and 9AM on the network, with West Coast updates to follow, which usually meant staying on until 11AM—a double-overnight shift! On the way home, finally, I'd stop at the gourmet grocery store, pick up something nice for dinner, and then when I got home I'd try to grab a short nap, put on a cute outfit, and get ready to greet Jim at home with dinner to kick off the weekend.

I wasn't the only one waiting for the weekend. We had a young and slightly beleaguered nanny working for us, Kathi, and she naturally wanted to get off duty as early as possible, especially on Fridays. By the end of the week she'd had enough of our kids and our schedule. She was relatively inexperienced, but she had an incredible heart and she loved my kids, and that was enough. I could have used much more help, but we could barely afford just the one sitter, so I raced home to relieve her—wanting Kathi to be fresh and revived by the time we had to start things up all over again on Sunday night.

It was a household held together by the thinnest thread. I see that so clearly now, but at the time I don't think I really noticed. Who had time to notice? We were barely functioning—until the moment I let it all fall apart. What happened on this particular Friday would not have happened if all these fatiguing factors hadn't already been in play. If I hadn't bent to the pressures—real or imagined—to get back to work. If I had been more like myself—instead of this overwhelmed, overextended working mom with a little too much on her plate, a little too soon after having a baby and moving to a new house and returning to an impossible schedule. If I had been on top of things, instead of swallowed up by them and reeling.

Our run-down Victorian had three floors, and the nanny and the kids were usually up on the third floor so as not to wake Jim at night. It's like they had their own little world up there— a wonderful setup, really. As soon as I came home, I sneaked into my bedroom to see if I could find at least a little bit of sleep—but, alas, I couldn't drift off. There was just too much going on. Too many of those spinning plates in the air. I lay still and quiet for an hour or so, hoping at least to recharge my batteries, and then when I thought I'd had enough I bounded up the stairs to the attic two at a time to see my girls. I was especially anxious to get Kathi off the clock. This taking-care-of-a-second-baby business was still relatively new to her, and I didn't want her to be overwhelmed just yet. There would be time for overwhelmed later, I thought.

Emilie would be taking a nap, I knew, like I should have been, but I figured Carlie would be up and ready to play. In fact, I could hear her as I took those stairs. For some reason, I was talking, moving, thinking a mile a minute when I stepped into the babies' room. Still very much in racing mode. Trying to accomplish a dozen tasks with just a half-dozen motions. I collected Carlie in my arms and reached into my pocketbook to pay Kathi while she filled me in on the girls' day—who ate what, and when; who had napped, and when—and we went through our hurried handoff ritual just as we had a dozen times before. In the back of my mind I kept thinking, *Let's get through this quickly so Kathi can get home and I won't feel guilty about working her too hard.*

Then, still zipping around like a wild windup toy, I moved toward the stairs. Not looking. Not thinking. Not paying good attention to any single thing. Just talking, and barely pausing to take a breath. Kathi and I were all squared away, and I turned to head back downstairs—only I misjudged the top step. *With my infant daughter in my arms!* The moment I did it I realized I'd set off a disastrous sequence of events. Next thing I knew, I was in midair, flying down the staircase. My back crashed hard against the middle steps, which meant I'd shot right past the top four or five. Somehow, Carlie was pressed beneath me each time I landed. Somehow, I managed to hold on to her, but she'd slipped to where I must have fallen on her little body when I came crashing down to the bottom. It happened in a split-second, but the realization of what had happened seemed to take an excrutiatingly long time to play out. From that midpoint thud on my back, I rolled and tumbled the rest of my way to the bottom of the stairs, making whatever feeble attempts I could think of to keep from rolling my big grown-up body onto Carlie's newborn frame.

I think I screamed. Not in pain, but in agony over the thought of my poor little baby girl. In my head, I was screaming. In my head, I was flashing forward to every inconceivable worst-case scenario, because Carlie had barely made a sound. Just a small squeak. I knew this was bad. I knew from the noise she made, and the way she landed. My first and only thought when I came clear was for Carlie's head. How seriously was she injured? How had she landed? I knew firsthand how hard we had hit, so I knew the answers couldn't be good. A sickening feeling of dread came over me. Her head was my immediate worry. Anything else, like a broken arm or leg, we could handle. It would suck, don't get me wrong, but it would heal. It was the thought of a head injury that had me terrified. What I couldn't see.

I knew we had to get to the hospital. There was nothing to think about, nothing to consider; it was my new reality, that's all. *Get to the hospital. Immediately.* Just as I was figuring whether to call 911 or to rush Carlie to the emergency room myself, I heard her make another tiny, high-pitched squeak. My entire body responded physically to the sound, and it washed over me that she really had been terribly hurt. That tiny, helpless, horrifying noise.

Kathi was just as horrified as I was, just as frantic. For all I know, she had the same sick feeling. She had seen the whole thing. She had heard the high-pitched squeak. I didn't have to ask her to stay with Emilie. Of course she would stay. I just grabbed my car keys and placed Carlie in her seat as gently as I could and raced to the hospital. I shouldn't have driven in such an agitated state, but I didn't think we had time to wait for an ambulance. The hospital was just a couple of miles away—I'd be there in the time it took to call 911. I cried as I drove. I prayed. I chanted, "Please make her okay. Please make her okay" like a mantra. The more I chanted, the faster I chanted, the louder I chanted . . . the more likely it would come to pass. My eyes darted back and forth from the road to my rearview mirror, catching glimpses of my baby girl and thinking while I was praying. *Pleasemakeherokay. Pleasemakeherokay.* It was all on me. That was what I was thinking, most of all. That this had happened because I'd been too fried and frazzled to carry Carlie down the stairs without tripping over my own damned feet. Because I'd been determined to take on too much, too soon. That's what it all came down to, in my racing imagination. Me, grabbing wildly at absolutely everything in such a greedy, transparent, selfish way. Maybe I was a monster. One of those horrible *career women*, worrying way too much about my network news job and not nearly enough about my own baby daughter.

I had deserved to fall. Of that I was certain. But Carlie didn't deserve any such thing.

I didn't think I could ever forgive myself.

I pulled up in the emergency room lane and spilled out of the car like a crazy woman. I flagged down one of the triage nurses and said, "I fell down the stairs." As if that would explain the enormity of what we were facing.

The nurse pointed toward the waiting room area and said, "You'll have to sit down, ma'am."

I said, "No, no, no. You don't understand. I fell down the stairs *with my baby*. On my baby. She needs to be seen." Then I held Carlie out, like a kind of offering. Or maybe an explanation.

I'm sure I was the picture of desperation, tears streaming down my cheeks, my face all twisted up in anguish.

Finally, it registered with this woman that we were in need of serious and immediate attention, and we were whisked inside. Someone took Carlie from me and started looking her over. An-

other someone started asking me a bunch of questions and looking me over. I was a complete, inconsolable wreck. Carlie was being examined right next to me, and I could see her the entire
time, but I kept asking, "Is she okay? Is she okay?" As if there
could have been some magic answer to erase the horror of what
I'd done to her.

They took her away for a brief moment to do a scan. The
emergency room doctor was concerned about a head injury,
that's all. That was my concern, too. As far as I could tell, nobody was checking for any other injuries, but there was a lot
going on just outside my view, so I couldn't know for certain.

Underneath my frenzy, I kept thinking about how I could
possibly bring myself to tell Jim what I had just done. I was
dreading the conversation. How could I face him? How could I
face myself? How could I face *anyone*? Me, the mother! The
one who is meant to keep this wondrous child from harm—not
grab her from the safety and comfort of our hired nanny and
throw her down the stairs. What kind of monster does that to
her baby? Who else was there to blame?

Finally—mercifully, incredibly—one of the emergency
room doctors came to tell me that it looked like Carlie was just
fine. There was no apparent head trauma, he said. The scan had
come back negative, and with this good report I calmed down
enough to look Carlie over, and she did seem okay. Just some
bumps and bruises, like me, but mostly okay. That said, I remember not fully *feeling* this moment. My heart continued to
race, so fast I could feel it. My nerves were still raw and these
few words of relief did nothing to calm them. Not really. I
couldn't completely convince myself that these medical profes-

sionals were telling me the truth, or that they knew what they were talking about. It didn't add up. I replayed the fall in my head. From the way we'd careened down those stairs, two and three and six at a time, it seemed almost impossible that she was okay. But I desperately wanted to believe that this was the case, so I accepted the report from the doctors and tried to feel good about it. I also considered the fact that I hadn't slept for more than two hours at a time in five days. Surely that was coloring my view, keeping me from seeing the situation as clearly as these trained professionals. I was numb with physical and emotional exhaustion. And so I thanked God that medical experts were on the scene, doing their thing, weighing in with this wonderful news.

As I drove back home from the hospital, I allowed myself to think I'd just received the biggest wake-up call in the history of bad parenting. I'd been too beaten-up by my emotions to show any outward relief while we were still in the hospital, but here in the car I could finally smile. And sigh. And cry all over again—this time with tears of unbelievable relief and happiness and sweet, blessed gratitude. And yet, tears of joy notwithstanding, there was this gnawing worry that kept coming back. Instinct was kicking in, and my gut kept throwing everything into question. Was I totally run-down or does a mother know? A mother knows, I decided. Even when it cuts against the medical opinion of the entire emergency room staff. And as soon as this thought came over me, it's like the car suddenly filled with this big, dark vibe, telling me that something was wrong. That maybe Carlie wasn't in the clear just yet. We were just a couple of hundred yards from the hospital parking lot, and suddenly there was this argument going on inside my head, back and forth: *She's okay. She's not okay.* Maybe I was still so shaken by what had happened that I couldn't lose all these worst-case scenarios and accept that everything was all right. Or maybe I was just depressed and anxious and guilty, and that's why I couldn't let it go.

I went back and forth in my head like this on the five-minute ride home, and as I pulled in to our driveway I leaned over the front seat to look at Carlie again, to quadruple-check that she was okay. As I did, she let out another one of those tiny, creepy yelps. It wasn't a cry. It wasn't even like she was fussing. It was just that squeaky, high-pitched noise from before—and it struck me again as a bad, bad sound. So I raced inside with Carlie and called Jim. It was the first time I'd spoken to him since the fall, and I couldn't put it off any longer. I needed his take on this. I needed *him*.

I said, "I think everything's okay, but Carlie and I had a bad accident. The emergency room doctor says she's okay, but I'm not sure. She seems a little off."

He said, "Off how?"

I said, "Off. I don't know, just *off*. She just let out a little cry, and it sounded wrong to me."

I told him the story—the short version. The unbearable, unacceptable long version would have to wait, along with whatever recriminations might come my way.

He said, "Call the pediatrician."

So I did. The doctor told me how to lay Carlie down on the bed and examine my baby on her phone commands, but as soon as I placed Carlie on her back I could see that she wasn't moving like she normally moved. Her head was lolling from side to side, almost imperceptibly, and her legs were limp and unresponsive. In fact, she wasn't moving at all from the neck down. Usually, she'd be kicking and bucking in this position, but her lower body was limp, like a rag doll. And her eyes weren't following me as I crossed her field of vision. They were open, but she seemed to just be staring blankly, at nothing.

At the pediatrician's directive, back we went to the car—even more gingerly this time, because whatever was wrong or broken with little Carlie, I didn't want to make it worse. I drove those few miles to the hospital as if the road were paved with eggshells. By the time I arrived, I was hysterical. If I'd been frantic on my first trip to that emergency room, I was now exponentially so. I was crying, distraught, in an obvious state of panic. Jim was on his way to meet us there, but it might take him hours. I was on my own.

This was about where I lost any composure I had left, as I described in the opening few pages of this book. The well-meaning hospital staffer, the same person who'd checked us in less than an hour before, was trying to put me through all these procedural paces, and I just lost it. I'm not proud of my behavior that afternoon, but I won't shrink from it, either. This was me, out of control. I can still hear myself, speaking madly in a low, guttural voice at the unfortunate hospital orderly in my clutches: "You !&*&@#!-ing take this baby back there now or, seriously, I will !&*&@#!-ing kill you!"

I calmed down—a little—as I followed Carlie into the examination area, where the doctors saw immediately that something was wrong, because they couldn't get her to move either.

They hadn't tried poking her with pins on our first trip to the emergency room, because the focus had been on her head, but now they started talking about bringing in spinal cord experts. Now the concern was that her back might be broken, and she was surrounded by a swarm of worried doctors. And there was no room in that swarm for me.

I had to get out of the way and watch from outside as the team of doctors and nurses and technicians poked and prodded Carlie and discussed what to do. They strapped her flat on a board. As they bound her tiny arms and legs with tape, I felt my eyes welling with tears. I felt the tears rolling down my cheek, my neck. Soon, my shirt was damp, because the tears would not stop coming.

When I tried to take my mind away from how badly Carlie had been hurt, my thoughts only got darker and darker. *My baby might be paralyzed. Because of me.* I stood off to the side, just a few feet from where the doctors were examining her, cradling my purse in my arms, where Carlie had just been. Wishing I could turn back time. I couldn't get Jim on the phone to fill him in on what was going on and get him to talk me through these desperate moments. The weight of responsibility was pressing down and down and down on me. It's like I could feel my eyes sinking into their deep, empty hollows. My skin turning pale. My blood running cold.

I don't think I've ever felt so helpless and hopeless in my life.

Carlie was taken in for an MRI, and I followed behind, unable to do anything for her. The imaging technicians draped her little body with a protective lead blanket and slid her inside a big tube. It looked like the machine was about to swallow her up, and I kept bursting into tears again at every new pitiful sight. The thought of my baby, alone, underneath all that noise. I had to leave when they were ready to start the exam, and as I stepped into the hallway I could feel all the energy being drained from me. Like someone had pulled a plug and all my thoughts and strength and emotions would now just spill onto the hospital floor.

The doctors ordered several types of scans, and each time there was an interminable wait for the results. They were telling me nothing because there was nothing to say until the results were ready. With each scan, the gravity of what was happening sunk in a little deeper. I'd been leaning against the wall, sobbing. And then I wasn't. I'd melted facedown onto the cold linoleum.

The only clear memory I have of that terrible wait was a dreadful exchange with a patient who happened by—a large woman, meaning to be helpful, I guess. She had been watching me. She knew my baby was inside the imaging room. She'd seen me struggling, despairing out loud. She leaned down to where I was on the floor and said, "Your baby's in trouble. You need to get her out of here right away. This hospital sucks."

If I'd been inconsolable up until that moment, this tossed-off comment pushed me to a whole new level. I couldn't think of a thing to say to this woman in response, so I said nothing—and in the long silence that followed I discovered deeper hopelessness and haplessness. *This hospital sucks* . . . The woman's words just hung there in that hallway, reminding me of everything I'd done wrong and signaling everything I'd continue to do wrong. I couldn't even get Carlie to a decent hospital. Our experience on the first trip seemed to back that up.

It took Jim a couple of hours to get to us, which was just short of forever, but in all that time we still had no conclusive word on what was wrong with Carlie. It helped a little when Jim finally showed up, but I couldn't look at him. I was too ashamed. In fits and starts, I managed to tell him the rest of the story, how I screwed up. He tried to talk me down from all that guilt. It didn't help, but it was good that he tried, good that he didn't beat me up about it any more than I'd beaten myself.

Finally, after five hours, I was able to be with her. Five hours! An absolute eternity.

Then a doctor came in to tell us that Carlie was indeed broken—but it was not her spine. She had a big break of her upper right femur. The thigh bone. Unusual in an infant, he said, because babies are so nimble and bendable. Her little body had gone into shock, which was why she'd been unresponsive earlier.

I don't think there's ever been a mother in the annals of emergency room history so overjoyed at the news of her child's broken leg. I was very nearly jumping up and down and clapping my hands together. Sobbing ecstatically now. Chanting, "Her leg is broken! Her leg is broken!" Like we'd just won the $10 million Powerball jackpot. It completely felt that way, that we'd won our daughter's future back. She'd be fine. Maybe not for a couple of weeks, or even a couple of months. But fine eventually. Nothing mattered more than that. It was truly the best news I'd ever heard in my life.

And then, an unexpected hurdle: Carlie's diagnosis put me under suspicion of child abuse, because broken femurs in babies almost never happen, at least not in quite this way. I might have anticipated this turn—I was a reporter, after all—but it caught me by surprise. They'd have to send someone down from Child Protective Services to question me, and I remember not thinking too long or clearly about this. It was something to get past, that's all. I had nothing to hide. I was so tired and worn down and angry at myself, that the investigating agent actually seemed a bit worried—I was practically turning myself in, going into extensive detail about what a terrible, reckless, irresponsible mother I was. In the back of my mind, I was thinking, *Where are the handcuffs? Put them on. Arrest me. Take me to jail right now.* For all I know, I might have said these thoughts out loud. And do you know what? If it had been up to me, I would have made that deal in a heartbeat—a simple broken leg for a guilty plea to whatever child abuse charges they wanted to throw my way. They could have locked me up for the rest of my life, if it meant Carlie would be okay. I deserved to be treated like a criminal, because what I had done was criminal in my mind.

I made such an effective and compelling case against myself, it's a wonder the woman from social services didn't cart me away. I didn't spend too much time thinking about what might or might not happen as a result of that inquiry. It didn't matter, because we'd been given this giant second chance, and for the first time since I'd taken that careless first step from the top of my third-floor landing all those hours ago I allowed myself to believe things would turn out all right. Probably not right away, but soon enough.

Poor Carlie still had a bad patch ahead of her. We all did. First, we had to transfer her to another hospital, and it took hours and hours, with one glitch after another. I rode in the ambulance with Carlie, and it felt to me like all the EMT types on board were staring at me, wondering what kind of ogre allows something like this to happen to her kid. *Stare me down all you like,* I wanted to say. *As long as you fix my kid.*

She was in traction at the hospital for about five weeks, and wore a body cast for another eight weeks after that. In the beginning, Carlie was lying with her head at the foot of the bed and her feet up in the air at the head, her broken leg pulled away from her body by a string. It looked really uncomfortable, but she was the cutest, bravest little baby, smiling ear-to-ear. Her fat delicious face lit up the ward of variously sick children. The hospital was under renovation and the pediatric unit was filled with all kinds of cases, from children on their deathbeds to those with mild illnesses. One little tiny baby next to us came in one afternoon, completely covered with red and blue marks, and by midnight the machines she was hooked up to started beeping loudly. Within seconds she was surrounded by doctors and technicians; within minutes, she was not breathing. They took her away. I kept my hand on Carlie the whole time, thanking God for her life and her health.

I was no longer nursing Carlie, of course, but I still felt the need to be with her. And there was still no sleep. I couldn't leave my baby in that hospital all alone, so I stayed with her, catching a couple quick winks in the chair by the side of her bed whenever I could. I didn't go to work, of course, so that washed away whatever goodwill I'd managed to build with my early return from my maternity leave just a couple of weeks earlier. It's like I never went back at all, which only reinforced my thinking that this accident didn't have to happen.

Outwardly, the people at CBS News said all the right things. They wished me and Carlie well. They were appropriately upset and worried. But underneath their genuine concern there was once again the not-so-subtle message from lower-level producers that they needed me back behind that anchor desk. They made it pretty clear. They'd tried a bunch of replacements, they said, and none of them were working out—or interested in signing on for any type of long-term commitment.

Carlie's eight weeks in the body cast struck me as the saddest, most depressing piece to this ordeal. Carrying her was like holding a small wooden coffin. You couldn't really hug her. She was trapped in this cumbersome and constraining tube. It was terrible.

There was no physical therapy, because Carlie was so little and the feeling was that she would recover whatever pieces of her development she had lost by being in that cast. Remember, she didn't move for a very key period in an infant's development, so there was a lot of catch-up she needed to do—and she was so eager she was able to make up that lost ground fairly quickly.

Looking back, I think I did fall into a kind of delayed postpartum depression during and after our hospital ordeal. It was the accident, the pregnancy, the withdrawal from work . . . all mixed up together in a weird, uncertain way. I cried all the time, though I tried to fight it. And in the middle of this allover funk and despair, I started to think differently about my career. Work was no longer this wonderful, fulfilling aspect of my well-rounded life. Work was now the enemy. After all, it was work and ambition that had done this to us. To Carlie.

I'd had enough of the enemy—of *that* job. The thought of trying to balance that crazy *Up to the Minute* schedule again after the damage I'd done to my family . . . it was just too much. I was done. I told myself it was time to stay at home and back off on my dreams of being a career mom. Or, at least, a career mom punching the clock on that particular career.

This was the moment when I learned that it is best to marry a man who truly knows you, even when you don't know yourself. Jim's response to my decision was simple: "No." As if that one word was explanation enough. Just then, I couldn't understand his resistance. If I stayed at home it would have made everything much easier for him. If I stayed at home he would have dinner cooked, dry cleaning done, and a rested woman eagerly waiting for him when he was done with his own impossible schedule. Also, there wouldn't be the cost of childcare. I laid all this out for him and it must have been tempting. But he was thinking long-term, while I couldn't see past my own short-term guilt and doubt and uncertainty.

"You can't quit like this," he said. "I understand you want to stop, but not like this." He told me to give it six more months, promising to go into debt if necessary to get the help and support we needed—twenty-four hours a day, if necessary. He said, "You can quit after you get your sea legs back at work in six months. But not now, not like this. We just have to do this right. You have to feel like you really want to quit, not like you have to quit."

This wasn't just one exchange. We kept coming back to it. Jim said all the right things, but I made him say them over and over. I couldn't hear him at first. For the longest time while Carlie was recovering, I wouldn't even consider going back to work. It didn't matter what Jim said. There was my "depression" to consider, whether or not I recognized it for what it was at the time. I absolutely wanted to quit, but Jim knew how much I enjoyed my job. He knew how important it was to me, and what it would mean to our daughters to grow up with a working mother. He also knew how much I was struggling with what had happened, and the thought that something just like it might happen again.

And so he took control. He took out loans to hire another nanny so I could get the rest I needed, and all the support we needed around the house. We hired a night person and a day person, which gave us round-the-clock care, which just about bankrupted us. We were completely broke. There was nothing in our bank accounts at the end of each week. Our house was in desperate need of repair. We had no furniture. We didn't really have very nice clothes, other than what I needed to wear for work. We let so much go because all we cared about was having the kids "staffed." To protect them from *me*. That's a hard thing for me to admit, even all these years later, but that was the truth. I could hold my children, I could love them, I could kiss them, but I could not be trusted to care for them for long periods of time while working overnights and being so limited on my sleep. I was shaky, frail. I didn't trust myself—especially after that fall down the stairs.

When you don't sleep all night, you can't think—or, at least, you can't think clearly. Add to that another sleepless night, and then another, and then another. Put together months and months of those nights, and then you have a baby on top of that; your brain literally doesn't function very well, and your body doesn't function too well, either. Anyway, that's how it was with me, and that's why I fell down those stairs. I wasn't in sync, and that's why I didn't trust myself to be alone with my children because I was not physically able to completely care for them. I could love them, but I could not care for them.

And so with all of this backup now in place at home, I agreed to go back to CBS and see what things looked like there after six months. In that time, I vowed, I'd start looking for a job with a better fit. A day job. A local news job. Cable. Something. It wasn't that I didn't want to work at all, I realized. We both knew I was wired to work. I just didn't want to work this job, with these hours.

Jim was amazing. A lesser man would have taken the stay-at-home wife option in a heartbeat. No question, my career added another layer of strain on our household. Another schedule to juggle. A burden. It would have been so much easier to have me at home, and at this point in my life I would have jumped at the opportunity as though it was a grand promotion.

But Jim knew what he was doing. He insisted that I stay true to who I was—and vowed that together we would do it right. No cutting corners.

So that's what we did. We set it up so the house could run efficiently in my absence—and even in my presence, because I needed my sleep to keep up with that killer overnight schedule and the daytime hours of job hunting. I went out on weekends to do stories for the *CBS Evening News*. I was trying to get noticed—at CBS, and anywhere else. And after a couple of months I realized I was really hitting my stride. It got to where I was able to fill in on the Saturday *Evening News* from time to time. I was once again in a position to say yes to anything they threw at me at the network—not because I was afraid I'd lose my job if I didn't, but because it's what I wanted, and because my husband had so inspired me, and given me the time and freedom to live and work and be a journalist. And because our household was functioning again. It was still grueling, but I stopped trying to be everywhere, doing everything. I let our sitters stay with our children all day if I felt I needed to catch up on sleep. It wasn't perfect. I was far less present as a mother, but the babies were loved and cared for and in no danger of flying down a flight of stairs.

In time, we even found a way to laugh about my failures as a parent—about *our* failures, I should say, because Jim kept insisting it was on both of us, what had happened with Carlie. I might have been the one who tripped and fell, he always said, but we were both responsible for ignoring the tension and the exhaustion and the craziness that set me up for that fall.

Our Christmas card that year was a family photo taken

while Carlie was still in traction, with the rest of us dressed in scrubs. The inscription said, "Happy Holidays, from the Parents of the Year." A little bit of dark humor from some of our darkest days, presented with the hope that there were better days ahead.

FIVE

Turning the Page

TELEVISION IS A VISUAL MEDIUM—much more so for women than for men. This in itself is not breaking news, but it's worth emphasizing here. In the broadcast news business, there's a constant pressure for on-air "talent" to look good. It takes up a whole lot of our time—far too much, if you ask me. And yet, whether or not we choose to buy into it, our "look" is an important part of our package. It's just as important as our knowledge, our insights, our ability to tell a story.

It's exhausting trying to keep up with the latest fashions, hairdos, and makeup—not to mention paying attention to your figure. I didn't always do a good job of managing my image, especially early in my career. A part of me didn't know enough to know it was important. During most of my run at *Up to the Minute,* I looked haggard and worn and probably overweight. It was impossible not to look bone-tired. Plus, I overate to stay awake—an occupational hazard—and the fact that for most of my time there I was either pregnant or nursing didn't exactly inspire a contemporary look. Add to that the rinky-dink lighting in our fifth-floor studio, which was more like the lighting in my fifth-grade classroom than on a network news set: fluorescent, which highlighted our worst features rather than softened them.

In small measure, at least, my relative youth and my strenuous exercise regimen made up for some of these challenges, but I now think that every month that passed on the overnight shift added years to my countenance. It was a losing proposition, plain and simple.

Looks matter. They just do. They go into the toolbox every on-air journalist must carry. It's how we market and position ourselves on the air, and at the same time it's also how we sell ourselves to news managers and network executives, who often use their own subjective "tastes" or perceived demographics to make hiring decisions. I learned this firsthand, a few times too many. Sometimes managers are quite blunt about this; sometimes they are vague and evasive; always, they are inclined to make the "safe" decision and go with someone easy on the eyes.

Names and connections can matter, too. For better or worse. I realize full well that I might never have gotten the call from CBS so soon in my career if I hadn't been the daughter of the former national security adviser. My dad's name ended up opening a few doors for me, no question. But the same name that helped me would also come back to hurt me at certain key moments along the way. In any case, it was always up to me to power my way through those doors, and to make double-sure not to overstay my welcome once I was inside. There was never any hiding from who I was, or who my father was, although from time to time people might challenge me on one of my father's positions and jump to the conclusion that it was my position as well—forgetting, perhaps, that journalists are supposed to be objective.

In fact, this small piece of name-brand recognition nearly ended my career before it even got started. It was when I was still toiling on the overnight shift, anchoring *Up to the Minute* under the watchful eye of our executive producer, Tom Bradford, just before Carlie was born. I always had the sense that Tom had really wanted to hire my dad but had to settle for me. He never said as much, but it was transparent. When he interviewed me for the job, he kept the focus on foreign policy—certainly not my strong suit, but I winged it. Once he hired me, Tom kept booking all these foreign policy interviews for me to do—and it seemed overly impressive to many CBS News producers that I had been to the White House and Camp David. I certainly didn't flaunt this association, but it was there for all to see. It got to where the producers acted like they were doing me a favor whenever my night's work included an in-depth interview on Russia or on NATO expansion. They all thought they were playing to my strengths—or, at least, to my *name*—but I dreaded those segments for exactly that reason.

In all modesty, I suppose I knew a little bit more than most general-assignment types on matters of politics and world affairs, owing mostly to osmosis, but it really wasn't my thing. It certainly wasn't my intellectual focus or lifelong passion, the way many people assumed. Quite the contrary. In fact, I was so out of my element in this area that I worried constantly I'd stumble so badly during one of the interviews that my bosses, the interview subject, and the viewers at home would all recognize that in my case the apple fell extremely far from the tree. I sweated my way through every single foreign policy segment they threw at me, and put my "vamping" abilities on full display. To no good result, I'm afraid.

Still, my father's reputation preceded me. I'd always suspected that the buzz in the newsroom was that I didn't get the job at CBS because I was Mika from Hartford, who was easy to look at and quick on her feet, not to mention a pretty good generalist who was comfortable on camera. No, there was a good chance I got it because I was Mika *Brzezinski* from Washington, DC, the daughter of Zbigniew. It was a package deal; when you got me, you got my dad, once removed. I did nothing to encourage this view; in fact, I made it clear that I couldn't touch my father in this area, but the connection was hard to ignore. It was important to Tom Bradford, I think, because he believed it vested me with a certain amount of credibility—credibility I didn't necessarily deserve, but since this was the world of television we could all content ourselves with the learned truth that imagery works in many ways.

For the most part, I navigated this mostly harmless association with as much honesty and humility as possible. However, there was one time when it jump-started one of the most discomforting moments of my career. Tom decided we would produce a two-hour *Up to the Minute* special on the fiftieth anniversary of the Central Intelligence Agency. He asked me to help book several former CIA directors to appear on our show in a roundtable format, with me as the host. Our Pentagon correspondent, David Martin, would be assigned to sit beside me to lend some authority to the proceedings—but again, with a last name like Brzezinski, it would fall to me to do most of the pontificating. It was my show, for good or ill. My ball to drop.

As high-concept specials go in the overnight network-news game, this was a bit of a reach for our little show. Still, everyone thought I'd be perfect in the moderator role—I suppose on the unsupported theory that because I could book the guests, I could certainly manage to interview them as well. And not just any old interview would do, mind you. I would have to display my comprehensive knowledge of agency history, and offer my insights into the CIA, and on and on. In short, I'd have to out-Brzezinski my own father.

Unfortunately, I could do no such thing. Not even close. And I seemed to be the only one at CBS News who dared to recognize this. To make matters worse, the show was slapped together in less than a week—no time at all when you consider all the research and preproduction that goes into a special two-hour broadcast. And this was before my new and improved, fully staffed household arrangement. When would I prepare for this roundtable discussion? How could I possibly bone up?

To complicate matters, these former CIA directors were all my father's friends: Stansfield Turner and James Woolsey . . . giants. I'd been around people like this my entire life. In fact, I'd been around *these very people*, and I knew there was no way I could hold down a two-hour panel discussion with some of the leading minds in intelligence and foreign policy and *not* make a fool of myself. For five or six minutes, one-on-one, I could likely get by—but a two-hour dance? There was just no way. I tried to convince myself I could pull this off, to kind of psyche myself into it, but the apprehension began to build as I took the train down to Washington to tape the show. The plan was for us to use the *Face the Nation* set, and for me to sit in Bob Schieffer's seat, which made the whole prospect even more intimidating. Me? On the *Face the Nation* set? In Schieffer's seat?

Wow.

The show would be shot "live to tape," which meant there'd be no stopping and starting over if I screwed up—or, I should say, *when* I screwed up. I sat alongside the former CIA directors and David Martin, who did not look pleased. Actually, he looked disgusted. He was turned away from me, as if to say to his friends, "I am not with this person and I can't wait to get out of here." His body language made me nervous, because it signaled that he knew what I knew—that I was in way over my head—and he wasn't in the mood to save me from myself today. I tried to make some relevant small talk as we prepared for the broadcast, but he wasn't having any of it. It was clear to him that I was out of my element—and, soon enough, it was clear to Tom Bradford as well. He could see from the way that I was fumbling with my papers and stammering through my lame attempt at collegial conversation with David Martin that I was uncharacteristically nervous. He could see me moving my lips as I tried to commit my scripted introduction to memory—a trick of the trade that sometimes worked for news anchors, but certainly not, as I was now learning, for moderators.

At ten seconds to air, a voice chirped in my ear to begin the countdown to broadcast, and my stomach took a dip like I'd just soared over the rise on a roller coaster. It was all downhill from there: five seconds, four, three, two, one . . . The show open started to roll: "This is a CBS News *Up to the Minute* Special. "The CIA: Fifty Years Later,' with your host, Mika Brzezinski."

The red light went on and I froze. For a terrifying moment, I wanted to get up from Bob Schieffer's chair and run away as fast as I could. Instead, I tried to speak—and I was exposed straightaway. I couldn't even get the name of Stansfield Turner's latest book right. He'd just published a position-paper-type book called *Caging the Nuclear Genie: An American Challenge for Global Security,* and of course he expected us to plug it on the show. Such was the quid pro quo of television talk shows: *we'll scratch your back while you scratch ours.* But I botched the title right in my intro. Admiral Turner had been the CIA director during my father's tenure in the Carter adminis-tration, so he'd known me since I was a kid, but when I called his book *Caging the Nuclear Genius* he flashed me a look that made me feel like something he wanted to wipe off his shoe.

I thought I could recover and move on, but I couldn't be-lieve I'd made such a stupid gaffe. The more I thought about it, the more I stammered and stumbled. My face was hot with humiliation—and we only had another hour and fifty-five minutes to go! Things got worse from there, and the next hours were the longest of my professional life. I was intellec-tually overmatched. In truth, it was no match at all. I was ut-terly incapable of steering the conversation in any meaningful direction. For a two-hour panel discussion on intelligence, there wasn't a whole lot of it flowing from the anchor seat, I'll say that. I could feel David Martin seething in anger next to

me. I dared not look his way. He'd been placed there as my colleague, an "anchor buddy." How demeaning. In just a few minutes I'd done my level worst to live down to his low
expectations, and he was so appalled by the bubble-headed
fake-blonde kid sitting next to him that to this day I'm surprised he didn't stand up and leave.

God knows, *I* certainly wanted to.

It was a thorough disaster. The whole time, it felt like I was
taking off my clothes in front of the entire world. Sweat dripped
down my back and under my arms. I imagined my father at
home, cringing. Or drawing up papers to have me disowned.

But I got through it. I figured that the best way to hide my
clear lack of knowledge was to say as little as possible and get
these guys talking to each other, and to drag David Martin into
the conversation even though he wanted to be anyplace else in
the world but on that *Face the Nation* set with an idiot like me.
Then, at the end of these excruciating two hours my guests
shook my hand politely and made a quick exit. As I recall, not
a single one of them asked about my father. It's like we all
wanted to forget our past association, and pretend we hadn't
just taken part in such an insipid discussion.

When we aired the show later that night, in our wee-hours
time slot, there was hardly any discussion in-house. Virtually
no feedback—a classic non-event. Even so, I walked around
feeling like everyone at CBS News had now seen me naked. I
went home and wanted to hide out there for a couple of years,
my face in a pillow, and wait for everybody to forget what
they'd just watched, but the reality was that by the time I got

back to New York from Washington, everybody was on to the next big story. Nobody talked about the CIA special—not when I was around, anyway. For all I know, there was a steady stream of snickering behind my back over this train wreck, but nobody ever said anything to my face. This was an invaluable lesson. It taught me that I could grind my way through just about anything on the air. And that most people in this business are *not* experts. I developed a sense of how to prepare for an interview in a short period of time—and how *not* to prepare. No, I hadn't gotten through this CIA assignment with anything resembling poise or polish, but I did get through it. Somehow. Maybe not in the way Tom Bradford had intended, and certainly not in the way I would have liked, but now that it was behind me I allowed myself to draw tremendous power from this realization. I might be out of my element from time to time, but nothing was out of reach.

I may have been woefully unprepared for that assignment, but my biggest mistake was taking it on at all. Ultimately, that was the greatest lesson: be honest. It doesn't matter what kind of work you do, or what level you're at. Know your limitations. Know that it's okay to tell your bosses when you're in over your head. That's what I should have done on this CIA broadcast, but I was still trying to prove myself. I didn't want to let anybody down. Plus, I'd been on this huge momentum roll at the network. People in management were talking to me about the big future they envisioned for me at CBS News. I didn't want to do anything to put an end to that talk. I wanted to keep that momentum going. So I grabbed at a little more than I could handle and hoped no one would notice—when the better move would have been to take a step back and admit I wasn't up to the task.

They don't teach you this type of thing in college. It's a trial-by-fire sort of lesson: the only way to get it right is to get it wrong first.

I always appreciated it when I came across a news executive who'd give it to me straight. A classic example of this came during those uncertain weeks when I wanted to quit CBS News after the accident with Carlie. With Jim's support and prodding, I'd pulled myself together as best I could and gone back to work, but I was desperate to get off that overnight shift. I had an agent making calls on my behalf, but I also made some calls on my own, working my way through my Rolodex.

Soon I got a chance to sit down with a vice president at NBC News. It was a thrilling opportunity, even if it was more of a fishing expedition than a full-blown job interview, because there was no specific job on the table. The meeting was with a woman who'd interviewed me several years earlier, when I had that brief stint in Vermont, fresh out of college, so she had been following my career. I had a lot going for me. I'd been back on the air for a couple of weeks, and filing stories all across CBS News, and doing good work. I thought I looked pretty good physically, too—especially considering what I'd been through recently. But then, if you have to qualify or justify your appearance with a phrase like *especially considering*, it can't be good. It was all relative to what I'd been through. I was starting to get my self-esteem back—and being able to sleep a full five hours in the morning after work was a godsend. But despite these small victories, I was still a bit disheveled. I was about 15–20 pounds overweight and retaining water from just having a baby. I'd been many shapes and sizes over the previous six months, and my wardrobe hadn't exactly kept up with all these changes to my body type. It hadn't really kept up with the general public's sense of style, either.

Nobody at CBS News had said a word to me about my frumpy appearance. The message I got back from management was that they were happy to have me back, that's all. It took sitting down with this woman from NBC for me to get a vivid picture of myself. She said, "Mika, I think you're great, we like your work. But you need to worry about your health and your appearance. Seriously. Start drinking water. Lose some weight. Wear some clothes that fit. Spend some time on your makeup. And get a haircut. We can't put you on our air looking like that. I'm sorry to have to tell you this, but I want to give it to you straight. You look awful."

And she wasn't quite through with me. She looked at my outfit—a long, tight-fitting purple tubular skirt with a matching jacket. She said, "Seriously, who wears that?" Then she pointed to the bright red splotches on my wrist, climbing up under my jacket, and quite reasonably asked what was going on there. I quite reasonably explained that I had been out pulling weeds at our fixer-upper home, and that I had caught a vicious case of poison ivy.

She cut me off in mid-explanation. She said, "Seriously,

Mika. You're a great person. You're great on the air. But you're not presenting well."

She was right. I wasn't.

I walked out of there demoralized—but I had to admire that she'd told me what no one at CBS would say. I could do the work, but my persona—my looks, my demeanor, the way I carried myself—just wasn't selling it. It was harsh, but I needed to hear it, and I took the words of this network vice president to heart. More than that, I took them as a challenge. I escalated the *let's-take-care-of-Mika* program Jim had suggested at home to red alert. I made a conscious effort to drink more water. I watched what I ate. I got a great new haircut. I went out and bought expensive clothes with money we didn't have. I became my own round-the-clock stimulus project. If it's true that you have to spend money to make money, then I would be living proof.

I worked on my "makeover" for months, until I was so pleased with the results that I asked the folks at CBS to take a new picture of me, to replace the head shot they used in publicity stills and in the CBS News hallways, where they hung huge portraits of the "faces" of the network news division for all to see. Soon, I noticed people stopping and staring at my new portrait on the wall, wondering what had happened to Mika. Wondering in a good way, although, of course, the compliments had a double-edge. I even heard someone wonder if I'd been replaced, because they couldn't recognize the attractive young woman in the spot where my photo used to be. A few of these surprised comments came from some high-level managers.

People who had been instrumental in hiring me. This was a stunning turn, I thought. I really must have looked lousy!

In the new and improved Mika photo, I posed with my arms crossed, with my snappy new haircut and an expensive, lush-looking, wine-colored Nipon suit. I got a copy of the photo and put it in an envelope, planning to send it over to the woman at NBC News.

To show I was a good sport, I slapped a Post-it note on the picture that said, "Is this any better?"

I thought the photo and the self-effacing note were a good way to keep a dialogue going, and to demonstrate to NBC that I was serious about wanting a job and open to their suggestions about my appearance. But as I was on my way out to the post office I couldn't find a pen in my kitchen to address the big manila envelope. I knew the picture would sit on my kitchen counter for days if I didn't get it out the door right away, so I grabbed one of my daughters' crayons—bright green—and wrote on the envelope in big green letters without really thinking about it.

When my package arrived at NBC, the vice president's assistant almost threw it away, thinking it was another inmate mailing, but the name over my return address stood out. She thought, *Wasn't that person just here recently?* She remembered signing me in, so she took the envelope to her boss, who tore it open and looked at the picture.

The NBC vice president called me immediately and said, "Yes, Mika. Better. Much better. Not sure about the green crayon, but you look great." Then she told me she had some big news, but that I shouldn't get my hopes up just yet. They were auditioning for a daytime talk show they had in the works, to be hosted by three women. She said, "We already have an idea which way we want to go on this. In fact, we've basically made our decision. But come in anyway, if you can."

She had me at "daytime."

Let me tell you, I would have taken a gig at the Home Shopping Network if it put me back on a normal schedule. I didn't like that she'd said the three spots had essentially been filled—but then I realized she wouldn't have asked me to come in if she didn't think I could fit myself into the conversation. Maybe she wasn't entirely sold on the talent she and her colleagues had already selected. Maybe the three potential hires hadn't showed any chemistry as a group. All I had to do, I told myself, was make a positive impression, so I put all my energy into doing just that. And, happily, the audition went extremely well—so well that I was offered one of the positions a couple of days later.

The job was a spot on a show for MSNBC—the network's twenty-four-hour cable outpost—so in some respects it might have been another step back. At the time, it was almost unheard of in the industry for a broadcast journalist to leave a network anchor seat for a job on a cable station. But I had a different take. Yes, my photo would come off that wall at CBS News; and yes, I'd be downshifting from network news anchor to a shared hosting role on basic cable; but where others saw a door closing on my television news career, I saw another one opening. I'd be working daytime, which meant a normal schedule and time to carve some semblance of a home life into my working week, so this alone was reason enough to make the change. I'd finally be drawing a full-time salary, which meant health benefits and a pension and all those good things. Plus, I'd be working for an outfit that seemed prepared to make a real investment in me, because in promoting this new show they'd also be promoting me as one of its hosts. And, as a kicker, NBC had already done a great job integrating its news division with its MSNBC and CNBC cable stations, so there was every reason to think the job might lead to opportunities at the parent network.

The show was called *Homepage,* and I was to share hosting duties with Ashleigh Banfield, the bespectacled darling of the network, and Gina Gaston, another rising star. At the time, Ashleigh Banfield was very much the "It" girl of cable news, and *Homepage* was being developed as a kind of star vehicle for her. Everybody knew her as the girl with the glasses—and soon, I would be known as the girl sitting next to her that you didn't really remember. It was written into our contracts that Ashleigh would open and close each show. I remember thinking this was such a meaningless distinction, and yet it was a telling indication of the producers' approach—Gina and I were supporting players. But I had nothing to complain about, and I don't think Gina minded too terribly much either. I had no need to be number one. In fact, I found it to be somewhat of a relief. Because of this setup, with Ashleigh cast as the star, I had a chance to develop an untapped talent—the ability to draw out and highlight the essence of an on-air colleague. It turned out I was a great sidekick. It called to mind the role I used to play at our family dinner table. Respond. Help the conversation along. Offer a contrarian view. It fit my personality, and I was good at it.

Little did I know that this talent would come back into play for me years later, during my second go-round at MSNBC.

Homepage was modeled on the *The View*, the hit Barbara Walters–led ABC talk show, we three female hosts would chat about issues and trends and the news of the day. Ashleigh was cast in the Barbara Walters role; she would be the maypole in our swirl of chatter. Our target audience was women, so we would mainly cover stories of relevant interest: organizing your life, managing your money, juggling home and career, and on and on. We'd be on from twelve noon to 3 PM, Monday through Friday, so I would have a viable, predictable schedule that would allow me to be at home each night with my kids. A dream job, really. Too good to be true. And yet here it was.

Predictably, my bosses at CBS News weren't too happy when I told them I was leaving. To celebrate my new job, Jim and I sneaked away for a mini-vacation. Andrew Heyward, the president of CBS News at the time, actually called me while I was on the beach in Florida to tell me I was making a big mistake. "It's cable, Mika," he said. "You're going to ruin your career."

I didn't think so. I just thought Andrew Heyward didn't want to have to plug that overnight hole, and that he was mad at me for leaving him in the lurch. And he was *really* mad. I had five weeks left on my contract, he reminded me, and he warned me that if I broke my contract I would burn bridges. He reminded me, too, that the television news industry was a fairly small, closed business, and that word would soon get around that I'd walked away from a commitment. It was his version of a "you'll never work in this town again" speech, and it wasn't all that persuasive. I just let him vent, pleased to have the buffer of all that distance between New York and Florida. There was nothing anyone could say to change my mind.

This big break at MSNBC came with another complete makeover. That NBC vice president called in a team of stylists, who took me on a whirlwind shopping spree. We went up and down Fifth Avenue, buying up the town—to the tune of $25,000, I was told, which struck me as an enormous amount for a new wardrobe. Then they took me to a high-end salon. It was nuts—almost like getting ready for a wedding. I didn't mind all the fuss and attention, but I was a little uneasy with how they wanted me to dress and wear my hair. It wasn't a look I would have chosen for myself, but I didn't think I could say anything. Nowadays, I'm much more in command of my appearance. It's now about knowing who I am, and dressing to what I know and what I want to bring across, instead of to someone else's ideal. But back then I kept quiet and let these professionals do their thing. I figured they knew what they were doing. They proceeded to outfit me in short skirts and high boots and extremely tight tops. They turned my hair a bright shade of blonde. Compared with my "before," my "after" looked great—that's what a complete makeover can do for you when it's coupled with some much-needed rest and pampering. But I didn't look like . . . *me*.

Who *was* I? Looking back, I know now that I wasn't sure of the answer to that question. I had no idea how vital "knowing who you are" can be to overall success.

We premiered less than a month after I signed on, so there wasn't a whole lot of time for me to get to know Ashleigh and Gina or for the three of us to begin to pick up on each other's rhythms. The plan, I guess, was that we'd figure it out as we went along, but the interplay among hosts can be a powerful foundation for a show like this, and there was no time to do anything but throw us all onto the set together and hope for the best. At least we all *looked* sensational—Ashleigh and Gina had had their makeovers, too.

In the beginning, we mixed a lot of substance and silliness, and we leaned a little too heavily on the latter. For example, we started out doing this forced bit with our shoes. To this day, I don't know how or why we did this, but someone must have thought it was a good idea. Ashleigh would welcome everyone to the show, and then she'd say something like, "Before we get started, let's check out our shoes!" Then Gina and I were supposed to scream, "Shoe check!" with mystifying glee. After that, the camera would pan to our shoes and we'd congratulate each other for looking so gosh darn fabulous, and off we'd go into the news. It got to where we started doing a formal segment called "Fabulous Shoe Friday." (Don't ask.) The rest of the time, we interviewed celebrities and we brought in experts to discuss issues and trends we thought might resonate with our stay-at-home audience.

Keep in mind, what passed for "news" on our show wasn't really news at all. It was gossip, lifestyle, advice, ill-considered opinion, and a whole lot of nonsense . . . all of it presented with a wink and a smile to show our viewers that we were *especially* interested in this stuff, because they were, too. It was much closer to acting than reporting, really. A lot of what we did felt stunted and contrived—basically because we were not developed enough as women or sure enough of ourselves to pull it off. Part of me realized this—but a part of me had no idea.

Very quickly, the three of us became friends. Gina and I grew especially close, and I remember telling her that *Homepage* would last two years, tops. We should use it as a stepping stone, but not depend on it as our future, I said. Looking back, I can't imagine how or when or why I'd become so wise, or jaded, or unwilling to trust in the moment. But I suppose I knew enough to appreciate the job for what it offered me right then: a day shift. A chance to breathe and try something new. But that was it. The format, the concept . . . it all seemed a little too forced for me to think we'd have a long run.

Once, they had me out on a segment on the merits and pitfalls of buying used cars versus new cars, and the idea was to pose me like a slinky car model on the hood of my Toyota Corolla. I went out in killer red boots and did what I was told, all the time thinking I was looking almost as foolish as I had that night on the *Up to the Minute* CIA special. That's what you do when you're just starting out in this business—and here I was, just starting out, all over again, draped across my car like some bimbo at the auto show.

I don't think I had a clear picture of who I was as a person or a journalist just yet. I was merely spinning my wheels and following the advice of a group of well-meaning and presumably talented people who may or may not have known what they were doing. They certainly didn't have the best interests of my career in mind, just what might work best for their show. And not to knock on Ashleigh or Gina—in fact, I remain friends with both of them to this day—but I don't think either one of them had a keen fix on who they were either. We were just following orders and trying to make the best of it, at a time in our lives when none of us were developed as caring, thinking, feeling, *experienced* women.

Sometimes, we managed to stumble on good, compelling daytime television in spite of ourselves, but for the most part we just stumbled. You wouldn't know it to look at the ratings, though. The show did quite well. We didn't light the cable world on fire, but the network was happy with our numbers, and we were developing a following. The concept was good, and the afternoon time slot was up for grabs, so we created our own little niche and started to fill it. We even hosted an hour on NBC for five weeks, immediately following *Today*, when *Later Today* was abruptly canceled and the network needed a filler.

Personally, I don't think I was ready for that job. Forget for a moment that the show itself wasn't fully formed when we launched. The key takeaway from that experience for me was that *I* wasn't fully formed either. I wasn't seasoned or confident enough to pull it off. I was a solid reporter, and a good interviewer. I was comfortable on camera, and able to deliver the news or a lead-in to a breaking story. But for a woman to thrive in the role of a daytime television host, and for audiences to respond to her, she needs to be pretty well grounded and absolutely sure of herself. She needs to be out there in a straightforward, unvarnished way, and to expect viewers to take her seriously because she takes herself seriously. Most of all, she needs to shoulder all the negative comments, very often over nothing much at all, and accept that people are checking out what she's wearing, wondering if she's put on weight, speculating on who she's dating (if she's single) and how long her marriage might last (if she's not).

I think back on where we are today, by way of contrast. All three of us are married now. Gina has triplets. Ashleigh, two young boys. I've got Emilie and Carlie, and my own wealth of new experiences. I bet if we came together on a show like *Homepage* today, it would be a gas, because for a format like this to really work in a sustained and substantive way, the hosts need to be more fully anchored and sure of themselves than we were at that time, at least in terms of our careers. That's why *The View* works so well, I think. From Barbara Walters on down, those women know who they are and what they're about. They've each got their own identity, and that's what comes across. They stand for something.

That wasn't me, just yet.

I was determined to grow into my new role, but before I could figure it out the game changed. News happened. Real news. Breaking news. The kind of developing, round-the-clock news we couldn't set aside for our sugar-soft version. *Homepage* was put on indefinite hold as the entire network switched to wall-to-wall coverage of the 2000 presidential election—and its whirlwind aftermath.

When the election failed to produce a clear winner, NBC News switched to twenty-four-hour coverage, vowing to continue in that role until the election was decided. It was the perfect opportunity for the news division to trot out its supplementary news model, deploying MSNBC and CNBC talent and time slots to offer complete coverage of a big story. ABC and CBS had no real cable presence, so they couldn't touch NBC in this area, which meant we essentially had the field to ourselves among the big-three networks. Only CNN could compete with us in terms of scope—and we were determined to give them a run. The news division called our wall-to-wall coverage "The Battle for the White House," and MSNBC ditched its entire slate of daytime shows in order to devote full attention to the story, from every conceivable angle. We had reports from the Bush camp, the Gore camp, the Supreme Court, the Florida courts, the Republican and Democratic national committees, the White House, the U.S. Congress, and on and on, all of it spiced with notes and comments from a merry-go-round of pundits and analysts.

Naturally, we needed some of our own talking heads to anchor these proceedings and file all these reports, so the network looked to MSNBC talent already on the payroll, which meant that I was on the air constantly. Ashleigh Banfield and Gina Gaston were dispatched on their own post-election assignments, while it fell to me to anchor a great deal of our coverage. Conveniently, I had some experience in this area, which was undoubtedly why they looked to me, and it was a tremendous piece of right-place, right-time good fortune. I ended up solo-anchoring a lot of our studio segments, as well as co-anchoring with Lester Holt, in addition to reporting and presenting sidebar-type stories of my own.

For some reason, I landed on the hanging-chad beat, handling a lot of the numbers, analyzing the recount, explaining the bizarre, byzantine business of Florida polling practices, and helping our viewers make sense of the various possibilities and likely outcomes of every conceivable scenario. The drill for a long stretch in there was I would stand at a huge dry-erase board and tally the recounts. It made for some gripping live television. A real story. These numbers would determine the future path for our country, so this put me front and center on one of the biggest stories of my generation.

The particular nature of my assignment was somewhat surprising, because math had never been my strong suit. I didn't have enough fingers and toes to keep track of the ever-changing vote count. I almost froze a couple of times, writing down all those numbers. There was one night when I was so tired from hours and hours of live coverage that I couldn't figure out if a certain set of numbers added up to 200 or 2,000 or 2,200 or 22,000. Somehow, I managed to fudge my way through. After a while, I took to keeping a little notepad in my lap or on the desk in front of me, out of sight of the cameras, and I'd rehearse my math on the dry-erase board. I'd write the numbers down during the commercial breaks and commit them to memory.

One day I looked up and realized that all the pseudo-news

and chitchat claptrap of *Homepage* was gone, and in its place was the kind of serious reporting I'd longed to do—on a breaking national news story that was shaping up to be one of the most significant chapters in our nation's history. For the first time in a long time, I felt connected with the work, with the content, with myself as a journalist.

I practically lived at our studios in Secaucus, New Jersey, for the run of our coverage, and it was thrilling. I missed my kids, but Jim had things covered at home, and I knew this schedule wouldn't go on forever. In the meantime, I was overjoyed to finally be doing the kind of work I felt I was meant to be doing—and doing a fine job of it, too. Brian Williams, who anchored our ten o'clock newscast, came up to me a couple days into our new assignment and said, "You're really shining, Mika."

We broke a lot of rules during that period, because nobody before us had ever been on the air in such an all-out way, covering such a complex, history-making story from so many different angles. One afternoon, we were trying to get the Broward County election commissioner on the phone, and Lester Holt just threw to me on the set and I tracked this guy down while America watched. Things like that never happened on television back then; typically, you'd have a producer make the call off-camera and report back with a quote or a sound bite, but here we thought we'd cut through the red tape and do it on the air instead. And it worked. We ended up with an incredible live hit, offering our viewers a behind-the-scenes glimpse at the voting controversy that none of the other news outlets had.

MSNBC just exploded on the back of that coverage. We pulled huge numbers—but more than that we made a name for ourselves as a news outlet. I felt very proud to be on the forefront of that. Proud *and* vindicated, because up until this time in my career no one had really thought I could do this kind of work. As far as most people in my industry were concerned, I'd come out of nowhere. In eighteen months, I went from anchoring an overnight CBS newscast that pulled nothing numbers, to hosting a cable-news chick show and being known primarily as the girl next to the girl with the glasses, to being the person on the most-watched news story in the country, counting chads.

Not exactly a direct path or any kind of meteoric rise, but I started to think that I'd finally arrived. So much so that Jim and I looked to put an exclamation point on my welcome career turn with our family Christmas card—an annual tradition that was fast becoming a cherished platform on which we could vent or sigh or shrug our shoulders at whatever had been preoccupying our attention for the past year. In December 2000, that meant a picture of the girls, decked out in opposing T-shirts: Emilie in a red T-shirt with "Bush" emblazoned across the chest; Carlie in blue with "Gore" in big, bold letters. Their expressions told the story. Emilie was smiling, cheering, while Carlie wore a big fat frown on her little four-year-old face.

The inscription: "Counting on a happy holiday."

My mother said I was always
a difficult child.

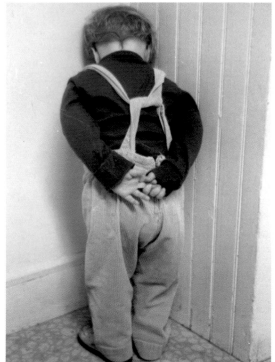

My mother in her
element.

I love this picture.

Ian, Mark, and me.

Long before *Morning Joe*, I spent my childhood trying to charm Morning Mom out of having to eat her cold oatmeal.

Christmas at the Brzezinskis'. My elegant grandmother, Emilie Benes (far right).

Me, the boys, my dad, and Tuffy atop Park Mountain
in Northeast Harbor, Maine.

My father and me
at the White House.

Jumping Strawberry.

Strawberry in the house
at Christmas.

We always found a reason
to bring the horse
into the house.

A pensive Zbigniew Brzezinski on one of my mother's signature pieces, "Bench in Flight."

Our only normal Christmas card.

From: Emilie, Carlie, Jim and Mika

Holiday Hugs!

Counting on a
Happy Holiday

Mika Jim
and the
girls

12/00

Christmas 2000. I was the official chad counter for MSNBC and our
Christmas card year symbolized the mood of the moment.

SEASON'S GREETINGS
— from —
OUR HOME to YOURS
2004

MAY YOUR NEW YEAR
BE FILLED WITH
MANY SURPRISES

Just for kicks we added a baby (friends were so stunned
they started sending gifts).

WISHING YOU A
Wonderful
Holiday Season

If you see mommy, wish her a
Merry Christmas!

First year of *Morning Joe* we mocked my long hours and constant travel
by switching me out with a replacement mom.

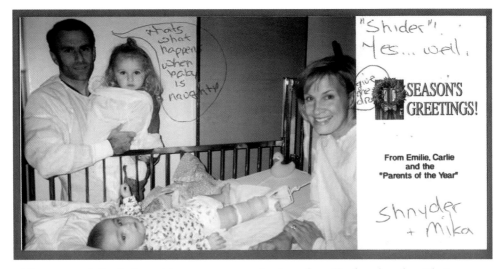

The year of Carlie's accident was a tough time for all of us but by Christmas we found a way to laugh with this card.

Anchoring CBS News *Up to the Minute* and in desperate need of a makeover (both inside and out).

SIX

Blink of an Eye

With the election decided and George W. Bush about to be sworn in as our forty-third president, MSNBC turned its attention away from Florida and back to its daytime schedule. It had been an exhilarating few weeks for everyone on the anchor desk—and for me personally, a chance to reinvent myself in the eyes of a lot of people in the business.

Homepage was now officially on the scrap heap, which meant I was once again uncertain about my career. The network had me doing general-assignment news and feature reports, and hosting various hours here and there, which was fine with me. Meanwhile, my old bosses at CBS News started calling again, which is a wonderful example of how fickle this business can be. CBS had been content to bury me in the Siberia of their overnight newscast for all those years, and then they tried to warn me about the dangers of wandering aimlessly in the desert of cable news. (They would say "cable" as if it were a dirty word.) All of a sudden, after I'd done some good, prominent work for one of their competitors, they started to see me as an attractive commodity.

I actually had lunch during this period with a CBS executive who said, "We never knew you could look that good, Mika." She said this without a trace of irony, and meant it as a compliment. At this point in my career, this did not faze me one bit. Of course I hadn't looked good when I was toiling on that late-night shift. How could I? The hours were terrible. The lighting was terrible. My makeup and wardrobe were terrible. I'd been so beaten down by that job it almost cost me my sanity, and my beautiful baby girl.

And yet somehow I looked a lot better to CBS News from this new perspective. Television news bosses love to feel that they're acquiring something or stealing something or creating something of their own. They want a leg up on their rivals. And you're even more desirable when a second news organization appears to want your services. If you're out of work, you're seen at best as a cheap alternative, someone who could perhaps plug a hole or fill a short-term need, but you're not someone who is likely to be brought in as the Next Big Thing. The same goes for someone toiling in a limited role. I might have been an asset waiting to happen, but CBS News wasn't about to promote me from *Up to the Minute* to a bigger role at the network, because to them I was just the kid reading the graveyard-shift news—on a day rate, no less. It took leaving for MSNBC and gaining some notoriety over there for CBS to look at me in a new light. I was a shiny new penny all over again.

At the same time, MSNBC wasn't moving too aggressively to keep me in the fold, because to their way of thinking I was already in the fold. If it's true that the heart wants what it can't have, then perhaps it follows that the heart takes for granted what it already has. As far as the cable network was concerned, with me already on the payroll the only questions were what I might do next and how soon I could start. Yes, my contract was nearly up and the show I'd been hired to work on had just been canceled, but to NBC News executives I was already in the asset column; they just had to find a way to get the most out of me. If they could do so without paying me any more money, or promising me a greater role in a new contract, then so much the better.

It was an odd little stalemate. I let CBS take me to lunch a couple of times and fill my head with talk of what a return to CBS News might look like. Once, Andrew Heyward, who'd told me leaving CBS was the biggest mistake of my career, actually came downstairs to meet me at the front door. He hugged me and said, "We'd love to get you back."

I thanked him, of course, because I was in the market for a new job, and genuinely excited about my prospects at CBS. I didn't begrudge Andrew for tracking me down on that beach in Florida. That was his job, just as it was his job to try to convince me to come back, now that my career was once again in play. Andrew, like me, has a great sense of humor about how this business works.

I ended up leaving MSNBC and re-signing with CBS News in an undefined role. On paper, the terms of my assignment were only slightly better than they had been when I was stuck on the network's overnight news desk, scrambling to get my stories onto all those different CBS News shows, but now they were built on the promises and enthusiasm of network executives who seemed to want to give me a shot at flourishing there. The short-term plan was for me to file stories for the *Evening News* and *The Early Show*. This time, the feeling was a little less like I had arrived, and a little more like I was back on track.

For the second time in less than a year, my career took a significant, unexpected turn on the back of a big, breaking story. It was my fifth day on the job back at CBS News, and I'd yet to go out on an assignment. I was still getting acclimated, reminding myself how things worked there, going through all those necessary motions with Human Resources, and learning my way around the phone and computer systems. I was also meeting with producers, trying to get them to put me to work, while they were trying to suss out the "cable girl" they'd just hired and what the hell she was doing there.

I loved my new little office. I loved that I was back in midtown Manhattan, after trudging out to the MSNBC studios next to a strip mall in Secaucus for the past two years. Those first few days back at CBS, I got into the habit of coming in early, trying to read all the newspapers and soak up as much as I could. I did this on the advice of my new colleague Byron Pitts, one of the network's top correspondents. Byron said, "Come in early and be the first to get the story." That was his thing, and I thought it made good sense, so I made it my thing, too.

It was a Tuesday. I sat down at my desk with my morning papers and my bagel, and then I noticed the monitor in the corner of my office. It was always on, like video wallpaper, but just then my eyes were pulled to a horrifying image: a plane had hit one of the towers of the World Trade Center. There was no accompanying audio, just the visual of the burning building—but that was enough.

I dropped my bagel and raced down to the assignment desk, where our national editor, Bill Felling, took one look at me and pointed to the door and said, "Go! Just go!"

That's all I needed to hear. I'm not even sure Bill knew who I was at that point, but I guess I had that hungry, pleading look of a reporter wanting to be let out of the gate. On my way out the door, I found a producer named Mike Noble who was also headed out on the story, and together we grabbed a cab and thought we'd be downtown in no time. Five minutes later, with midtown traffic at a complete standstill, we jumped out and decided we'd be better off on foot.

I said, "Mike, I hope you can run."

He said, "I'm a smoker."

I said, "Well, you're gonna get healthy, right now. We're running."

I kicked off my shoes and started sprinting, barefoot, all the way from West 57th Street to the World Trade Center. In all, it was just a couple of miles, zig-zagging in and out of traffic. The scene was intense, every step of the way. We took the West Side Highway, which was backed up like a parking lot. Clusters of people were standing alongside their cars, listening to their radios, their heads tilted toward the downtown skyline and the plume of smoke that swirled ominously over the lower tip of Manhattan. It was such a crisp, clear, brilliant morning, not a cloud in the sky—except for that massive billow of smoke from the North Tower.

Mike and I picked up snippets of what was happening as we raced past all those gridlocked cars, with their radios on and their windows open. At one point, we heard a bulletin that another plane had hit the other building. We just kept running. With the news of the second plane, though, I kept fixing my eyes on the eerie downtown skyline. I let my mind wander as I ran. What was I running into? Then I thought about Jim. I knew he'd be headed down there, too. We would both be in the middle of this.

I thought immediately about the girls . . .

It was one of the few times in our careers that we would move so recklessly in the same direction, toward such danger, such uncertainty. We hadn't spoken that morning since leaving for work, and yet I felt connected to Jim, as if we were feeling the same pull. Thinking of each other, in one way or another. I had no idea how he was, but I knew exactly *where* he was. I knew we were reaching for the same thing, and we were putting the same things at risk.

Most people in the CBS newsroom thought at first that there'd been a horrible plane crash. An accident, probably. I'd just assumed it was some tiny propeller plane that had flown off course, but now as I raced past those radio reports, I heard bits and pieces of bulletins about the type of plane, then about the other plane, and by then it was becoming clear that this was a coordinated attack. The whole way downtown, I kept thinking how crazy it was for me and Jim to both be heading straight to the disaster site, but at the same time the story was like a magnet. I was a reporter. I had to go.

I lost track of Mike Noble in the chaos, but somehow I got

to within five hundred feet of the South Tower, on Liberty Street, just before the police put up their yellow tape to cordon off the area. The police and the firefighters were still establishing their presence on the scene. Most midtown news crews had yet to arrive, stuck in the same traffic Mike and I had abandoned. The cell towers were all out, so there was a mad scramble of people looking for working pay phones. I got so close to the towers that when I looked up I had to tilt my head all the way back to see the smoke and fire about eighty stories above. It was a point of view I remembered from my very first visit to the World Trade Center—a real tourist's pose, only now there were no tourists, just hordes of frightened people, knitted together by unthinkable tragedy.

There, in the crowd, I ran into Byron Pitts—true to his word, first to the story—and we stood together in the dark shadow of the South Tower, looking up, wondering what the next moments would bring. It was such an unlikely, serendipitous encounter, given the pandemonium all around, but we were both grateful to have run into a familiar face. Together, we were the first reporters to report live from the scene for CBS News.

I stood next to Byron as we craned our necks skyward and took in the circle of fire high above us. I started to wonder how those on the upper floors could escape. Maybe a helicopter could rescue them from the roof. It was the only way, I started to think. It didn't cross my mind just yet that there would be no way out for these people. No solution, no mass rescue. But then, Byron started counting out loud. I couldn't understand why, until my brain caught up with what my eyes were seeing: small specks falling from the upper levels. At first I'd assumed it was debris. But then I knew. Byron was counting bodies. Human lives. People who had simply gone to work that Tuesday morning. Perhaps they'd taken the time to vote in the primary, or to enjoy the beautiful day. And now they were facing an impossible dilemma—to burn to death inside these office towers or jump to their deaths one hundred stories below.

The building started to teeter. Initially I thought it was an optical illusion, because we were standing so close. But within seconds the entire top of the South Tower began to crumble and cascade to the ground. I wondered immediately if my husband would be trapped in the pile of rubble instantaneously forming on the plaza level. My mouth fell open. Within seconds, a massive, roiling ball of debris was heading toward us like a 500,000-ton snowball barreling down a mountain, getting bigger by the second. I froze. For a dangerous beat or two it didn't even occur to me to move out of the way, but Byron took me by the hand and said, "We've got to get the hell out of here."

I was having such a difficult time processing the scene. If Byron hadn't pulled me away, I might have stood there longer.

We held hands and ran, through a crush of people, with the billowing ball of ash and debris just behind us. Surprisingly, I don't recall a lot of people screaming. It was just a massive crowd, on the move. Everyone just wanted out. Someone even said, "Excuse me," as he darted in front of me.

A long block from the Trade Center, we ducked inside a school. Already, a group of New York City firefighters had established a makeshift way station in the lobby. I started fumbling around, looking for ways to report on this story. There was a clothing bin for the poor, so I helped myself to a pair of boots. It took seeing that bin for me to realize that I was still holding my heels, clutching them tightly in my left hand. I threw them down, disgusted that I had wasted all that energy carrying my shoes this entire time.

Next, we went in desperate search of a phone, rummaging through the rooms like criminals ransacking an apartment. I finally found one, tucked away on a shelf, so then we started searching the walls for a jack. We plugged it in. When we lifted the receiver and heard a dial tone, it was like we'd been handed a lifeline.

I said, "Byron, we're in."

We called the newsroom. "It's Mika," I said. "I'm here with Byron . . ."

Within seconds, a producer was saying, "Standby, you're on with Dan . . ."

Dan, of course, was Dan Rather, who was manning the coverage from our studios on West 57th Street, and Byron and I took turns describing the scene and helping our viewers get a sense of what was happening. For a few adrenaline-tinged moments, I forgot about my husband, my kids, my life as I knew it up until this beautiful morning.

The only thing that was important to me right now was telling the story to Dan Rather—and to the world.

Luckily, the phone cord we'd found was about twenty-five feet long, so we could cover a wide area of the school lobby as we reported. Firefighters and rescue workers were streaming in and out of the building, which stood as a kind of oasis—a place to get a drink, or a chance to take off cumbersome headgear for a moment. When they saw us, though, with our live telephone line, they also started using it to send messages to their families. Many of them knew they would not make it home that night. I could see it in their faces. I could hear it in their voices and in the good-byes they were sending out over the airwaves:

Please, tell my wife I love her.

We had no camera crew at this early stage, so we used our words to paint the picture of what was going on along the ash-filled streets outside the school windows. But the words of the firefighters really brought the story home. They would take only a moment to talk with us, but for some of them it was a moment they felt they had to take, because it loomed as their last connection to the world. The anguish in their eyes gave them away, especially the veterans. They knew what they were facing. A sense of knowing that this was the end, but at the same time that this was what they had to do. They had to go back in.

I think of these men and realize there is no better use for the word *bravest*. They were the best of us.

Soon, Byron and I had worked out a loose system. I'd find a firefighter or police officer to interview and bring him back to Byron, who would put him on the phone to talk to Dan. Then we'd switch, and I'd take my turn on the phone while Byron went off in search of interview subjects.

The North Tower was still standing when we made our first set of reports. At one point, on the phone with Dan, I felt the school start to shake, like we were in the middle of an off-the-charts earthquake. Of course, I should have known what it was straightaway, but there was no frame of reference for what was happening. Dan cut me off, and started narrating what he was seeing on his studio monitors . . . as the North Tower began to fall. His voice was low and ominous, framed by what was happening all around me as I held the phone to my ear. The chaos and commotion that had gripped these streets just a few moments earlier was back again in full force. People were running for their lives all over again. Escaping the crush of steel and concrete and glass. And then, everything went dark. As if the windows of the school had all been shaded. I heard the clap of debris hitting the school walls, the sound of glass shattering as debris broke through the school windows. I hit the floor. The few firefighters who had been in the school lobby before the second collapse ran out into the oblivion . . . but there would be no call to answer. Nobody to rescue.

I started to panic about Jim. I'd been worrying about him all along, of course, but now he was all I could think about. I asked Pat Shevlin, the executive producer in charge of our special coverage, to have someone at the desk check in with Channel 7. Surely, I thought, someone at Jim's station would have heard from him or he would be on the air and I'd know he was okay in this once-removed sort of way. I didn't want to bother him, I just needed word. We were now several reports in, the second tower had fallen, and I had heard nothing.

Pat was back on the phone just a few moments later. She said, "Mika, you're on with Dan in ten seconds, and your husband is fine. He's going to be on Larry King tonight."

I started crying, but only for a split second. It was more like a yelp, because there wasn't time for more emotion. I had another report to deliver. Pat's bulletin had told me two things: one, Jim was okay; and two, something serious must have happened because he'd been booked on *Larry King Live.* These two pieces of information filled me with relief and worry, all at once, but there was no room for either emotion because Dan Rather was in my ear, pumping me with questions, and I switched back into reporter mode. What happened to Jim, I learned soon enough, was that he had been standing near the North Tower, doing a stand-up report, just as it started to fall. The resulting video captured the hell and frenzy of the moment, and that's why they wanted him on CNN, to talk about what he had just seen and narrate the dramatic video. I knew Jim wouldn't be too happy about this. It cut against his particular brand of journalistic integrity. This was a tragedy of epic proportions—and unlike most of the characters in our business, who might want to capitalize on their sideline role in this event to propel their careers, Jim wouldn't be interested.

A short time after this next report with Dan, I managed to get a call through to our nanny, at home with our two children. Emilie was just five and a half years old, and Carlie had just turned three, and I didn't want them anywhere near this story. I said, "Jim and I are safe, but the girls are to watch no television. None."

There, I thought, hanging up the phone. I was on the job, in the middle of all hell breaking loose, with no idea of what these next terrifying moments might bring, and I was still trying to mother, in what few small ways I could. What I hadn't counted on, though, were the endless calls to our answering machine at home, from well-meaning friends and family wanting to know if Jim and I were okay. The calls started early that afternoon and continued for the next several days.

There was one message, from a family friend, saying, "Mika, you poor thing. I'm watching you on television right now. You're wearing a gas mask. I'm so worried about you. Call and tell me everything is fine."

Days later, when I played back those messages, I realized my kids very likely heard them as they were being left on the machine, so for all I knew they'd been filled with worry anyway.

Back at Ground Zero, we were moving constantly. Day and night, walking around the wreckage of the World Trade Center, doing interviews, taking in the scene, and then walking back to the truck to feed video and talk to Dan Rather on the air about what we'd seen. This went on for days and days. I barely slept, but the story drove me. It drove all of us. I interviewed rescue workers, city officials, people who had been in those buildings, family members still desperate for word of their loved ones.

One downtown neighborhood became a living memorial to those who'd been trapped inside the towers. Family members stood in the streets with pictures of their loved ones. Every day, I'd interview grieving people clinging to these photos and pleading for help in locating their sister, mother, brother, husband, wife . . . still hoping that he or she was somewhere out there, missing, but soon to be found. I met so many people like this. They were locked in a moment, trying to fight off the next moment when they would realize the person they were looking for would never come home. These people drove me to keep going, day and night. I felt compelled to help them tell their stories, to give them a voice. I think a lot of us reporters felt that way. There was also a deep sense of personal guilt. At the end of this ordeal, I would get to go home. Maybe not right now. Maybe not this week. But I would get to touch, feel, and smell my babies again. And they would have me back, too.

Normally, I'd find ways to cope with long absences from home. Travel was a part of the job, so I'd learned to deal with it. I'd know my babies were being taken care of, and Jim and I would always do our best to make sure our schedules didn't crisscross when we were away on assignment, so that one of us could be home every night or every morning. But this was a completely different assignment. There was no timetable here. We would stay on this story as long as we were needed.

Whenever I called the house, once phone service had been generally restored, Emilie would say, "When are you coming home, Mommy?"

And I would say, "Soon, my little one. Soon." Then I'd hang up and think that soon couldn't come soon enough.

When I first saw Jim on the afternoon of September 11, it felt as if we had been separated for weeks. In fact, the two of us still can't agree on when this moment actually transpired. Jim is convinced it was that afternoon, right after the towers went down. I am convinced it was five days later. We can agree on *where* our meeting took place: on the West Side Highway, just past the CBS live truck. Jim was several blocks away when I saw him, outside the line of TV news vehicles. He remembers that he was with his crew, but I remember that he was alone. In any case, I ran up to him. My first instinct was to run to him and kiss him, which of course I did. Then I looked into his eyes, and it was as if I couldn't recognize him. I'd never seen that look on him before: detached, empty, dead, blank . . .

I was different, too, but was doing a better job of hiding it. Jim's face reflected the reality and gravity of the moment that had changed both of us. Nobody should have to see the things we had just seen. Just because we were reporting on these events didn't mean we were numb to them.

Our coming together like this was important, because it let me feel connected to Jim once more. We talked around what was happening, not *about* what was happening. There was nothing to say, really. It was too incredible, too unthinkable, too impossible to fathom. It's like we were coming at each other from a completely different place, and as we parted, off to meet our separate deadlines and commitments, I walked away haunted by our reunion on the highway. It erased some of the worry I'd been carrying since the first tower fell. Not all of it, but some.

It would be two and a half weeks before there was enough of a break in our coverage for me to go home and give my daughters a hug. That had been the other giant worry I'd been carrying that morning, and here it was almost twenty days later before I had a chance to reconnect at home. I went first to Emilie's school. Carlie was much younger, and I guess I thought Emilie would be more aware of what was going on, and more aware of our absence from the house, so my plan was to stop by her school and collect her in a quick embrace.

I hadn't counted on my emotions getting in the way.

I must have looked like a mess when I walked into that school. I hadn't had a real shower in weeks, and I hadn't slept more than a few hours at a time. One of the nuns saw me wandering around, kind of aimlessly, and she walked over to me. I probably looked to her the same way Jim had appeared to me, that first time I ran into him on the West Side Highway: disconnected, unreachable, confused.

"Can I help you?" she said.

I told her who I was, and that I was there to see my daughter.

"Is there a problem?" the nun said. She looked me over, as if to indicate that my very appearance was a sign of trouble. "Has there been a death in the family?" she asked.

I explained that I was a CBS News correspondent, that I had been at Ground Zero covering the story, and that I hadn't seen Emilie in almost three weeks. I told the nun that it was extremely important that I see Emilie and hug her and tell her everything was okay. It all seemed perfectly reasonable to me, but this nun saw it a little differently. To her, of course, Emilie was just fine. After all, Emilie had no reason to think everything *wasn't* okay. She was just five years old, and perfectly happy playing with her little friends. She knew it wasn't Emilie who needed to see me; it was *me* who needed to see *Emilie*. And so this nun had every reason to think this wasn't such a good idea.

Still, she sent for Emilie—and fought back the urge to intercede when I raced to my little girl and nearly collapsed in tears. Right there in the hallway, in the middle of the school day, I started to cry in my five-year-old's arms. Poor Emilie didn't know what to make of her mother. Or maybe she didn't give it much thought. But it wasn't really about Emilie, I realized. I shouldn't have been there, but I couldn't help it.

After an uncomfortable moment or two, the nun approached us cautiously and suggested that Emilie might want to return to her classroom. She approached at just the right time. The nun pried Emilie from me and helped me explain to her that everything was okay, and that Mommy was just having a bad day.

Then the nun handed Emilie off to a colleague—after which she turned to me herself and gave me a good long hug of my own. She asked if I was okay. In truth, I wasn't. I'd just emerged from the epicenter of our nation's devastation and despair, and I guess I was having trouble transitioning. I'd just seen parents dealing with the loss of their children, children dealing with the loss of their parents, and it was all just hitting me.

Jim and I had very different and separate reactions to what we had been through. I was pretty raw and emotional, at least when it came to reconnecting with my family and reestablishing our routines. Jim was a little more workmanlike. Because his station was New York–based, the reporters there were driven harder on this story than we were at CBS. For many more weeks after 9/11, he was still pounding the pavement, working to bring a different investigative angle of the tragedy home, every day at six o'clock and then again at eleven o'clock. He was barely around.

That meant it fell to me to make an extra effort at home. As soon as I could, I started trying to balance the kids' needs with Jim's needs, and the needs of my new job. At work, I turned on the charm, trying to dazzle everyone. I pushed stories hard and forged friendships quickly—perhaps a little too quickly—in an attempt to establish a zone of comfort to solidify my position there. I'd done good work in the aftermath of the attacks, but I didn't want to count on that to give me any kind of leg up. We'd all done good work. Our reporting from Ground Zero felt more like a responsibility than a feather in my career cap. So I set that work aside and thought I could now make my mark by becoming everyone's friend and being the best team player CBS had ever hired. Soon, my nickname at work became "Fabulous"—because I was super friendly, always smiling, always wearing colorful shoes. *Fabulous.*

I hesitate to share any more of our story from after September 11, out of respect for the thousands who perished in those attacks and the family members whose lives were truly shattered. Jim and I both struggled to find our footing after returning to our regular newsroom routines, but our struggles pale in comparison. For a long time it wasn't clear what normal looked like anymore, not after what we'd all been through.

I was busy "rushing" relationships to find and cement a place for myself at CBS. To his great credit and great good fortune, Jim had good friendships built over the years at Channel 7. But my husband was always cut a little differently from me in this regard. He's much more of a solid, serious reporter, with a long-term career at one place. With me, there was nothing really *genuine* about my workplace relationships, and I've tried to understand it. Over the years, I've found that the more competitive the environment, the more likely it is that your relationships are dubious alliances rather than true friendships.

The truth of my situation was this: in the world of network news, I was a piece of meat. I made the mistake of not getting this for a long time, investing workplace relationships with more intimacy and importance than they deserved. The question on everyone's mind was not what kind of friend I was— but whether I could carry the CBS News mantle and justify the faith my colleagues and bosses had placed in me. Oh—and how quickly and cheaply I could get the job done.

Every six months or so, I would request a meeting with Andrew Heyward to assess the progress of my work. I'd also do this with Jim Murphy, the executive producer of *CBS Evening News*, and Marcy McGinness, a vice president in charge of talent. I would use these meetings to see where I might improve and ask about opportunities for growth. Of course, the meetings didn't exactly occur in a vacuum. They were private, but everybody seemed to know about them, so I used to hear from fellow correspondents and producers about them. Everyone was surprised I had such access to these higher-ups, but I never saw it as any kind of big deal. I just picked up the phone or sent an e-mail asking these people for a few moments of their time. To me, it was about pursuing opportunity as if you deserved it. Selling it. Selling yourself.

At one lunch meeting about two years in to my second CBS News tour, Andrew Heyward suggested that I meet with Jeff Fager to discuss the possibility of doing some work for him. I listened dutifully but didn't really catch the name or recognize it. Andrew seemed to note that I was not overly impressed or even fully appreciative of his suggestion. I said, "Sure, I'd be happy to meet with him." And then I tried to move the conversation in a different direction.

I just assumed Jeff Fager was another in a long line of CBS

News producers who might or might not be all that interested in giving me an assignment. In fact, I didn't even hear his name correctly. I'd mushed it all together and heard it as "Jefaeger"— a last name, I'd figured. Then I went back to my office and asked one of my friends if she'd ever heard of some guy named Jefaeger, and she scratched her head, same as me. Then I asked another someone, and another, until finally I came across a friend at the *Evening News* who said, "Oh, you mean Jeff Fager?"

I said, "Yeah, I guess so. Who is he?"

"Who is he?" my friend said, incredulous. "Ummm . . . he's only the executive producer of *60 Minutes*."

Naturally, it got around that I didn't know who Jeff Fager was. It also got around that I was meeting with him— another mistake of my own doing. The buzz began to spiral out of control:

> *Mika is meeting with Fager!*
> *Who did she sleep with to get that meeting?*
> *She thinks she's so great, she pretends not to even*
>   *know who Jeff Fager is!*

My naïveté set in motion the nonsense that plagues every newsroom: the petty gossip and back-stabbing, the speculation and intrigue. We're reporters, after all, so our antennae are always up and out, listening for a good story. We invariably turn our professional skill sets on ourselves and our colleagues. The smarter move would have been for me to have gone back to my office and waited for the call from Andrew's office to set up the meeting. In that time, I could have looked up Jeff Fager online, or on the CBS News website, to find out who he was. Or I could have simply asked Andrew on the spot, when he mentioned it. It was a mistake on many levels. I was too trusting, counting on the confidence of my supposed pals. I was too needy, thinking my friends might like me more or feel more connected if they knew others were interested in my career. It shouldn't have mattered if "Jefaeger" turned out to be the producer of a webcast—it was nobody's business that I was on his radar, but I'd found a way to make it everyone's business. It came from a need to please, impress, and befriend that got in the way of appropriate professional behavior. What do I mean by *professional behavior*? I mean: Keep your head down. Let your work speak for itself. And while you're at it, have a modicum of self-confidence and self-respect.

When our post-9/11 coverage began to slow, I started going out on general assignment. Before long, I was filing strong, compelling pieces, and even anchoring the CBS *Evening News* from time to time. I was determined to get noticed. Truth be told, it helped that I'd made a little bit of noise while I was over at MSNBC; the CBS News brass hadn't brought me back to sit on my hands; now I had a bit of a name and a reputation—a career!—so they couldn't bury me.

I worked hard to become the go-to reporter on the desk, and producers from all CBS News broadcasts were at last starting to pay attention. I was signing on for every story they threw my way—a tactic that can take you a long way in a network newsroom, even though in the end it can only take you so far. Later on, I would realize that I was diluting the quality and style of the very talent I was working to develop. At the time, though, I only saw opportunity—everywhere I looked. *CBS Sunday Morning.* The *CBS Evening News. 48 Hours.* Even *60 Minutes II.* They all seemed to want a piece of me—and I gave freely.

There's a good news–bad news factor in being so agreeable and so versatile in a network newsroom. The good news is I got many opportunities to tell amazing stories. There was a two-part series on bipolar disorder in children for the *Evening News,* that took me to Clovis, New Mexico; Boston; Chicago; all over the country. (We actually won a Gracie Award for that series, which was a great big deal.) There was a *60 Minutes II* piece on some scuba divers who'd found the remains of a German U-boat off the coast of New Jersey, so we brought back some incredible footage. Most memorably, perhaps, there was a *48 Hours* story on an incredible group of women in Savannah, Georgia, whose husbands were all part of the same chopper unit in Iraq. The women got word together that their husbands' chopper had gone down and one of them had died. It was the most emotional piece. These women had been friends—they'd spent every weekend together since their husbands were deployed, just to bond—and when word of this crash happened they gathered at one of their apartments, knowing only that one of their husbands had been killed. It was such a horrifying, harrowing moment of discovery for these women, and we managed to capture it for our viewers.

No one day was like another, and each new assignment

was shot through with excitement and possibility. I was always getting on the air.

The bad news was that I spread myself so thin I didn't have a chance to develop any kind of niche or area of expertise. And I set myself up to be on the receiving end of a whole lot of finger wagging and head shaking and interoffice rumor mongering that would in many ways mark my second tenure at CBS News. And it all seemed to follow the typical arc of a CBS newswoman's career:

Look, she can anchor breaking news without a
   prompter!
Let's have her be available for all breaking news.
Look, the shiny new penny can do quirky, funny
   stories!
Let's have her do kickers.
Look, the shiny new penny can do serious
   investigations!
Let's have her do in-depth series.
Look, she can anchor, too!
What a shiny, shiny penny!

I wasn't about to argue. When asked, I delivered. I developed such an in-house reputation for being overbooked that one of the CBS hairstylists dressed as me for Halloween. She wore a blonde wig and walked around with a cell phone to her ear. That was her "Mika" costume. I didn't know whether to be flattered or insulted—but I was ripe for caricature, I guess. I never turned down an assignment. I usually had several going at once, and more requests on the back burner. My BlackBerry rang night and day with calls from producers wanting me to work on this or that piece, and I relished the positive attention.

It was a heady time, but I didn't want just to please everyone at work. I made it a special point during this period to meld my family life with my job. It was all connected, I thought. I lived to work, and I worked to live, so it made sense to let the two aspects of my life cross paths. I began to bring my kids to shoots. Carlie came with me to *Sesame Street* when I interviewed Elmo for *Sunday Morning*. Emilie would come to know Betty, Karen, and Mary Lou as my favorite producers (and real friends) and talk with them on the phone all the time. The girls loved coming to my office on days when I would anchor, to play secretary at my desk. They knew Paul and Bilgi in makeup. If I was anchoring on a Sunday night, chances were Emilie or Carlie would be hiding under the desk, tickling my feet as I read the news to millions. It felt to me like I was balancing this act of blending family and work with precision. My female colleagues seemed genuinely impressed at how I was managing it all.

I started to think that everything was coming together perfectly. I was developing solid working relationships with producers all over that newsroom, or so I thought. I'd managed to make or enhance a reputation for myself as someone who could handle a breaking story. And yet for some reason my career prospects remained unclear. That is, until the summer of 2004, when I was in line for my first big-time network contract. Dan Rather was slouching toward retirement as the *CBS*

Evening News anchor, and the lines of succession were starting to form.

It would be another couple of months until the infamous "Memogate" debacle that ultimately sealed Dan's fate at the network—and, in so many ways, mine—but already there was talk of how to replace him, and where the other pieces might fall as a result. I listened in to all that talk with great interest.

There were a number of opportunities that opened up for me around this time. One of these was a spot as a *60 Minutes* correspondent, courtesy of Jeff Fager, which was absolutely huge. Granted, it was on the *60 Minutes Wednesday* broadcast, where Dan was said to be taking on a broader role, but I'd be working under the same proud banner as Lesley Stahl, Mike Wallace, Morley Safer, Ed Bradley, and all those other CBS News legends. Another big break about to come my way was a fairly regular anchor spot on the *Sunday News*. John Roberts, the longtime *Sunday News* anchor, was said to be one of the front-runners for the main anchor seat, so in the game of musical chairs that typically accompanies such shuffling, there would be an open spot. Already, I'd been filling in for John, because he'd been filling in for Dan.

All this hard work and interoffice speculation seemed about to pay off as my contract came due, and people started to tell me I was in line for a bit of a windfall. And, sure enough, that's what happened. There was a big raise. There was the assurance that I would take over as *Sunday News* anchor when and if John Roberts moved on to the main anchor chair. There was the promise of working on *60 Minutes Wednesday*. I would also contribute to *CBS Sunday Morning* and the *CBS Evening News.* In short, there was everything I could have wanted at that stage in my career—and much more than I ever expected. It was a "pinch me" moment—so, of course, I pinched myself, to make sure I wasn't dreaming. I had run and lobbied and "befriended" my way into a primary role at CBS News.

And then I fell back to earth.

A few months into my new contract, the newsroom was buzzing with a new story. It gets that way sometimes, when something of moment is about to break. It's in the air, and all around. Dan Rather was said to have landed a big one. None of us had any idea what the story was about, but we knew it was big.

I tuned in at home, expecting fireworks. I microwaved some popcorn and settled in bed to watch. The kids were asleep. I was terribly excited. None of us outside the story's circle had any idea what the report would be about, but we knew to watch. Now that I was a *60 Minutes* correspondent, the success of the show could only mean good things for my career, so I watched with a real rooting interest.

The story turned out to be a *60 Minutes Wednesday* report throwing President George W. Bush's service in the Texas Air National Guard into question. The report was based on the discovery of several documents that seemed to suggest the president had received preferential treatment in being assigned to the National Guard, which enabled him to avoid being drafted and having to serve in Vietnam. There was some interesting new information, but there wasn't the surprise factor of a typical *60 Minutes* investigation.

Journalists often depend on their gut feelings to make decisions. My news gut told me something was wrong, very wrong, and everything was about to change. Within hours of the broadcast, bloggers were weighing in on the Internet, suggesting that the memos alleging the president's preferential treatment had been fabricated on a computer, long after the period of time under review. Within weeks, the report had gone from an embarrassment to a mess to a firestorm of controversy—Memogate—and, it seemed, the entire CBS News organization was thrown into question. Already there had been talk about life at CBS News after Dan Rather. But now that talk intensified. Now everything was on the table. Now CBS had to take a step back from its own story and admit that some of the documents it had based the story on were probably not authentic. We were all under the bus with Dan and his producers on this one. People lost their jobs. The network conducted a long investigation that distracted all of us. It was a black eye for CBS News.

By October 2004, it was announced that Dan's final broadcast would be the following March, but that he would remain with CBS News as a correspondent for the *60 Minutes* franchise.

There was a sweeping change of CBS News management, and somewhere in the sweep the people responsible for promoting me left the network. Andrew Heyward was phased out—and so was Josh Howard, the executive producer of *60 Minutes Wednesday*. All because of Memogate, it appeared. I could feel my support slipping away every time I walked into that news-room. My "friends" all seemed a bit distant. Those producers I'd aligned myself with, all over the newsroom? The ones who'd sung my praises? Who'd taken the time to connect with Emilie and Carlie? Producers with whom I'd spent days on the road, on planes and trains, talking about our lives, our problems, our com-pelling stories? They wouldn't even look me in the eye if they had the bad fortune to pass me in the hall. Understand, I didn't have a thing to do with the President Bush/National Guard piece, but it would seal my fate just the same. My future had been very much tied to Dan Rather's future and the future of the execu-tives who had been swept out with him. If *60 Minutes Wednes-day* struggled as a result of this mess, then I would struggle. John Roberts might not ascend to Dan's anchor chair, and I might not take over on the *Sunday News*. There were all these dominoes, falling just the wrong way.

Was I about to be fired? At this early juncture, there was still no reason to think so. But my role at CBS News was now up for grabs again. There would be new management in place, a whole new slate of producers I'd have to impress and show what I could do. I'd have to justify my big salary all over again. This thought alone didn't faze me, because I was ready to do it all over again, this time with more experience, more confi-dence. I was aware I might have to take a step back given the shake-up at the network. I'd done that before. I could do that again. But I didn't get that chance. One day, I realized I wasn't getting any more stories. All those calls—*Can you do this? Can you do that?*—just stopped coming. I couldn't get on the air. I was pitching stories left and right and getting nowhere.

I was left to dangle, anchoring the news on Sunday nights (because that was in my contract) and twiddling my thumbs the rest of the week, until finally I went to see Sean McManus, the new president of CBS News. *60 Minutes Wednesday* had just been canceled, and I wanted to talk to him about my future with the network.

I didn't know Sean McManus at all. He hadn't hired me. But he could certainly fire me, so it made sense for me to seek him out to see where I stood. I'd received a call from ABC News about the overhaul of their *Nightline* flagship, so I thought it made sense to take my pulse at CBS while I still had one.

After some small talk, we got down to business. I put it to Sean McManus directly. I said, "I love it here. I love my colleagues. I love the work. But I'm well aware that things have changed. If you need me to get out of the way, I will. I understand how these things go. If you want me to leave, we can discuss this."

His response surprised me. "No, Mika," he said. "You're great. You're going to have a big role here. We just don't know what it's going to be." He asked me to pitch him ideas, to help him redefine my job. Was there a particular beat I wanted to cover? He seemed to really want me to work on this with him.

So that's what I did. I imagined all these different roles. I pitched myself as an environmental correspondent, a women's issues correspondent . . . anything I could think of to stake out some new territory of my own. I was open to anything. I would even have taken a pay cut, if anybody had asked—my salary was at least twice what a typical correspondent was making. I knew that if my role was redefined, my salary would need to be revisited as well. That's how much I loved being a part of CBS News. That's how sure I was of my ability to reinvent myself at the network again.

I continued to anchor the *Sunday Evening News*, but now it felt to me like I was the holding-pattern option in the anchor chair. Now it felt like they were using me in this role only because it was in my contract. Like I was on the way down instead of up. I was nowhere. Every now and then, some producer would throw me a story, probably because there was no one else available, but for the most part I was idle, sitting in my office with nowhere to go, nothing to do. My "friends" would walk by and look the other way.

And then, when I was headed back to New York after a rare location piece in Washington, DC, I got a call from my agent. He said, "I just got word from Sean McManus. He wants to see you. Brace yourself, Mika. I'm afraid you're about to get some bad news."

I said, "What's the news?"

He said, "I really don't know, but it can't be good, him asking to see you like this, the way they've been using you."

I said, "The way they've been *not* using me, you mean."

Curiously, the network had just announced the signing of Katie Couric a couple of weeks earlier, to fill the anchor seat that had been held on an interim basis by CBS News veteran Bob Schieffer. What it meant was that there were all those dominoes again, lining up against me. All kinds of scenarios bounced through my head, that whole trip back to New York. On the way, I figured out that the reason they had kept me around all these months was as some kind of contingency plan.

At best, I had been plan B, I realized, and now that plan A had worked out and Katie was coming on board five nights a week, there was no need for the network to trot out a woman to anchor on Sunday nights. Especially if that woman was also a highly paid *60 Minutes* correspondent. Especially now that *60 Minutes Wednesday* had been canceled. Especially if you're Sean McManus and the woman you were considering for the role wasn't even your hire.

Just then on that trip back to New York it made absolute sense to me that I'd be the next piece to fall. Of course, I'm not so full of myself to believe that Katie Couric, cohost of NBC's *Today* show, had replaced me in the pecking order of CBS News; she was ten times bigger than me. But it seemed clear that her hiring meant there was no longer any room for me. Not in the budget, anyway. If they took me off the anchor chair and rerouted me toward the general assignment pool, I'd be a big fat waste of money.

My agent was right. The news was bad. The only good thing about it was that I'd seen it coming.

"It's not going to work out," Sean McManus said.

Just like that. *It's not going to work out.*

It was May 2, 2006—my thirty-ninth birthday. I said, "So, I'm supposed to sit here and do nothing, until we hit some window in my contract and you can release me?"

I'll never forget, sitting in Sean McManus's office that afternoon, taking in the news. The sun was shining through one of the big picture windows. Half of his face was in shadow. It was almost surreal, like the moment was being played out in a badly lit movie and I was on the wrong side of a tired cliché.

I wouldn't go easily on this. I fought him. I asked him what it was that I'd done wrong. He said I'd done nothing wrong. I didn't think that was a fair response, so I put it to him again. I said, "Why?"

He hadn't offered up a reason, and I felt I deserved one. I knew it couldn't have been the quality of my work. It couldn't have been my attitude. It couldn't have been anything I might have done, or anything I might not have done. And sure enough it wasn't.

Sean McManus simply shrugged and said, "It's just subjective. I'm really sorry."

Subjective.

I repeated the word to myself a few times, trying to understand how it applied to me. I wasn't sure it did. Sometime later, I heard there was another high-level executive who just didn't think I was all that attractive. After everything I'd done, all the good work I'd managed and the hard-won skills I'd developed, it came down to whether I was pretty enough to be on the air in a prominent way. Whether that played into this "subjective" decision, I'll never know, but it hurt to hear. At around this time, the same executive was interviewed about making hiring choices. He wrote, "I know it when I see it."

When asked what he was looking for in his next nightly news anchor, the suit said, "It's like porn. I'll know it when I see it."

I read that and thought, *Hmmm.* Isn't it nice, to have your work likened even in this sidelong way to hard-core porn?

As I said, it was surreal. And now it was also infuriating. To be let go so arbitrarily. I was shaken and upset. But at the same time, it was also uplifting. At least, that's what I told myself, as I left the fading half-light of Sean McManus's office. I told myself I didn't need these CBS News executives to validate my worth. I didn't need them to define me. The way to play it was to turn a negative into a positive. I'd been going nowhere at CBS, ever since Memogate, but with such a big contract there had been no real incentive for me to go out and shake things up and try something new. Now there was every incentive to do just that, and as I walked out of CBS News that day I allowed myself to think how prophetic I had been, all the way back in high school. I'd known all along that my career would end at forty.

I was a year ahead of schedule.

SEVEN

Lost . . . and Found

EVERY WORKING MOTHER grapples with the feeling that she should be at home when she's at work—and at work when she's at home. It's the classic career-woman balancing act, and in my case I felt it all the more because of my unpredictable schedule at CBS. No matter how hard I tried to get it right, it always felt like I was tilting in the wrong direction.

Some of us are simply wired for work. It's in our bones. Some of us are wired for family. And some of us are wired for all of it. That's one of the things I immediately admired about Sarah Palin, when she stepped onto our national stage during the 2008 presidential campaign. Her wiring was on full display. Forget about her politics—as a woman, she was intriguing to me. One of the first women of my generation who showed no guilt or anxiety about her ambition and desire to contribute. I really liked that about her. I respected her for never once seeming to be torn about where she should be: governing or campaigning, out to dinner with her husband or at home with her kids. She found time for it all, and yet she never set this out or highlighted it as anything special or abnormal. It was who she was, that's all. She stood before us as a fully formed career woman, and she moved forward as a parent, a partner, and a politician in an uncompromising way. That spoke to me. She turned out to be a political disaster, and her own worst enemy. But even today you get the sense you could put any obstacle in front of her and she would find her way around it with a smile on her face, and maybe one of those annoying winks, too.

I respected that Governor Palin found the time to raise such a big family, and then stand by them during the campaign, without a blink of embarrassment at the controversies that surfaced in their wake. She held her head high and kept her family right by her side. No apologies. No excuses. No explanations, even. Just unflagging support for each other. Come what may.

I was disappointed that she turned out to be incapable of intellectually rising to the challenge. It reminded me of similar areas in my own career on a smaller level. I felt the same admiration for Michelle Obama and Senator Claire McCaskill and many of the fantastic women I had a chance to interview. These women were true to themselves in every aspect of their lives, and willing to take on unprecedented challenges to live their ideals. It's what I always wanted for me and my family. Challenge. A partnership in marriage where two people push each other to grow intellectually. A family that motivates one another as individuals and comes together as a team. The ability to focus on one aspect of your life one day and turn that focus in an entirely different direction the next. My parents had done that so successfully. My mother especially. She, too, was wired for all those roles. Maybe those wires crossed from time to time and it looked like everything would short-circuit, but she figured it out before long.

My mother was the model I'd tried to emulate throughout my career, particularly during my second go-round at CBS, when my girls were getting bigger and it felt to me like we were all starting to hit our stride. In a lot of ways, I succeeded. In some, I fell short. In a few areas, I wasn't even close, but as they grew up my kids started to understand what things were like for me, and how I was different from some of the other mommies they knew. I wasn't a total anomaly in our neighborhood. A lot of women worked. But my schedule was a little more frantic and all-over-the-place than most. The career I chose and the way I chose to pursue it meant my time was not my own. When I was on the clock, I'd never know what they'd have me doing, or how long they'd have me doing it. My kids would wake up in the morning and get ready for school, and then they'd think, *Hmmm, wonder where Mommy's going to be today* . . . Or maybe they wouldn't think about me at all—and that was okay, too.

They had their routines, while I flitted in and out. That was their norm. During some big stories, the only place they would see Mommy was on television, but they always knew I'd be home . . . at some point. Still, there were times when they really missed me, and when I really missed them. And, inevitably, I missed out on many of their rite-of-passage moments—but then, we would balance that out by creating these wonderfully different memories and experiences for them, whenever those opportunities arose. I'd miss my daughters' birthdays from time to time, but then I'd make it up to them by throwing a party a couple months later, or doing something spontaneous and nutty, like throwing an impromptu water balloon party. As I write this, I'm missing Carlie's elementary school graduation, so there's a constant tug and pull between what I need to be doing at work and what I'd like to be doing at home. It's all about sending the all-important message to my girls that I'm with them in spirit if I can't be with them in person, and fully experiencing the moments when I *can* be with them. It's no different than a hardworking father who can't make it to each and every milestone in his kids' lives, and yet somehow women are judged for this. I'm sure there are people in my community—parents, teachers, and on and on—who shake their heads and question my priorities. For all I know, they might even question my love for my children, but I've stopped letting the second guesses of others add to my stress.

I looked to the example of my father, when he was serving in the White House and would sometimes be gone for many, many days. He'd always make it up to us with unique moments we could share together—like sneaking me off on a secret trip to Tunisia when I was fifteen years old. He had a meeting with Yasser Arafat, and I trundled along and took notes. Just me and my father and Arafat—surrounded by a dozen armed Palestinians.

In the beginning, when my girls started school and got involved in their own activities, I worried that I'd miss some important event or other. Parent days. Recitals. School plays. I'd put these events on the calendar, and then worry like crazy as the date approached, hoping some breaking news story wouldn't pull me away. But after a couple years, I realized all this anxiety was unhealthy for me and for them. I'd either make it there or not. I'd either be a present, available mother, according to the standards of school and community, or not. And the only judges I would answer to would be Jim, Emilie, and Carlie. I tried my best to tune out the biggest, most critical voice . . . the one in my own head.

Once, Emilie was performing in a circus at school. She was in third grade, and was terrifically excited. I had every intention of being there, but work kept getting in the way. I'd set it up so I could duck out early, told my bosses what was going on, but every time I tried to leave the building something would come up. All day long, I kept thinking about this damn circus. I had the best intentions, and I kept imagining Emilie's little face broadening into a smile when I showed up. But I'd also learned over the years not to make promises to my kids I couldn't keep, so I'd taken to saying, "We'll see." Or, "I'll do my best." The idea was that if I could make it to their special event they'd be happily surprised—which was a lot better than having to disappoint them, time and time again.

Still, it killed me that I might not be able to break away on circus day. The clock and the rush hour traffic were against me. I finally managed to leave, and took a car service home. I was cutting it close. The school was only about a mile away from our house. The whole way there, I was watching the clock. Fretting. Willing the traffic out of the way. And it was looking good. Not great, but good. The driver pulled up to my house with about five minutes to spare, and I raced inside, splashed some cold water on my face, took a quick glance in the mirror to make sure I didn't look too disheveled and harried and headed out the back door to my car. I had my keys in my hand, and I was good to go—but my car wasn't in the driveway! My entire body sagged. I'd had the whole thing choreographed and scripted, and now this . . .

Apparently, the car was at the local garage, where Jim had dropped it off to have the oil changed or something. We hadn't communicated—we *never* had time to cover everything. So I made a quick decision. It was only a mile, so I ran. Grabbed my bag, kicked off my heels, and took off. I was wearing a suit jacket and a skirt, jogging through my neighborhood barefoot, and I arrived at the school a short time later, glistening with sweat, my makeup running down my face. I looked like hell. I think I still had my shoes in my hand when I walked in the door, and everyone turned to look at me like I was a wet dog messing up the kitchen. I sat down, still catching my breath, and fixed my eyes toward the circus and acted like I was no different than any other parent in that room. I looked ahead to the small victory of the day that still awaited—Emilie's face when she saw that I was there.

Okay, so Emilie was too busy doing her somersaults to even notice when I came in, but *I* noticed. I felt a tremendous sense of purpose just being there. Knowing I'd done everything I could and that this time I actually made it.

Sometimes, Jim would represent us at these events. And sometimes, neither one of us would make it. That's just how it was in our house, and it had to be okay. Because if I worried or fretted over these things, I would lose focus. I'd become that woman who fell down the steps with her baby, again. I would have learned nothing from that terrible day. I would still be running ragged, plugging holes, and feeling like a failure. Trying to be everywhere at once.

As the girls got older, they came to accept that there would be times when we couldn't be there for them. We looked at this together, as a family. We talked about the challenges and benefits of our careers, and the girls participated in the trade-off; they found it exciting to be the daughters of two broadcast journalists, watching both of us on television. They might be upset or disappointed if we couldn't make it to a *particular* event or activity, but the big picture was always clear. Just as it had been for me when I was growing up.

Did I ever feel guilty about not being there all the time for my kids? Yes. Absolutely. But the guilt never came from Carlie or Emilie. It came from friends and family, some—not all—of whom thought they could figure things out for us. It came from the judgmental looks I'd get—real or imagined—from those really put-together mothers who managed to get to the circus ten minutes early instead of ten minutes late. But here was my reality: If I'm assigned to a story for the *CBS Evening News,* and I'm supposed to go to Parents Night and sit at my daughter's little desk . . . well, trust me, I'm expected to do that story for the *CBS Evening News.* The business makes that decision for you. I did what I could to stay on top of whatever was going on with my kids at school. I'd call their teachers. I'd e-mail. I'd catch up during off hours. Sometimes, this would involve some groveling, to get a private meeting before or after the public meeting I'd miss. But most of my girls' teachers were helpful and accommodating, most of the time.

That's how things went while I was at CBS—only now I wasn't at CBS anymore. Now I'd have to figure things out all over again.

It took a while to get my mind around being fired. For one thing, I stayed on for a while at CBS to fill out my contract. All fired up and no place to go—that was me. At first, it appeared I'd be staying on at the network for months and months, but I didn't have those months and months in me. Weeks and weeks . . . that's about all I could handle. It was humiliating, because there was nothing for me to do. I cashed my checks, twiddled my thumbs—it was hardly worth the commute time away from Jim and the girls.

I thought it was important before making my final exit to tell my girls what was going on. I'd put off the conversation for the longest time, because I'd allowed them to become so involved with my life at CBS. They knew my producers, my crew. They'd hung out on the news set. I'd thought this was a good thing—built on that take-your-daughter-to-work model. I thought that by opening up that part of my life to them, they'd be less likely to feel I was abandoning them during my long stretches away from the house. But I came to see that this was actually a mistake. I'd wanted my children to see what I was doing when I was away from home, to feel what I felt about where I worked. To get a little bit excited themselves about the things that excited me. But now that it all was being taken away from

me I realized that involving them with my workplace was probably one of the most selfish, self-indulgent moves in the annals
of working motherhood. Because it meant it was being taken
away from them, too. I hadn't thought of that.

I thought I was being sensible, integrating the component
parts of my life to enhance the whole. I was trying to be everything to everybody and I ended up being nothing, ultimately.
It was very public, very painful. Like a lot of women in our industry, when you rise through the ranks very quickly, you start
to drink your own Kool-Aid. You buy into the image your bosses
put out, and you allow yourself to think you're untouchable. I've
turned all the way around on this: I now feel strongly that the
workplace is for work, and the home is for children. On special
occasions, for good reason, my children might accompany me to
work. But that's it.

Carlie took the news a lot harder than her big sister. Emilie
was wonderfully self-absorbed, in her own little world—as all
kids should be. But Carlie felt things deeply. My plan was to
give it to them straight, with a positive spin. Simply put, I lied
to them. I wanted to protect them from the pain I was feeling,
so I tried to make it sound like good news. I sat them down on
the couch one afternoon and went into my act. I said, "Girls,
Mommy has something really exciting to tell you."

They snapped to attention—because like most little kids
they liked to hear exciting news. So I kept at it, in my practiced,
perky morning-anchor tone. I said, "I'm going to be leaving
CBS, and it's going to be so great. We're going to have so much
more time to spend together."

I was slathering on the enthusiasm pretty thick. They

looked at me like I'd gone stark, raving mad, because of course what I was saying had nothing at all to do with the Mommy they knew. Nothing to do with the role they'd seen me navigate at the network.

Carlie flashed me this stone-faced, disbelieving look and said, "No way! No way! You can't do that!"

And then Emilie, from her own entitled perspective, chimed in: "No way! You can't! That's the only reason the library lady likes me!"

I didn't exactly pick up on these little signals, so I continued with my charade—again because I thought I was protecting them—and tried to convince them of all the positive aspects of this new phase in my career. Carlie surprised me the most. She was quiet and withdrawn by the time I was through, but I didn't want to push the issue any more than I already had, so I let it go. I figured if she needed to talk about it some more, she'd find a way to talk about it some more.

She certainly did—the very next day. I got a distress call from Carlie's teacher, Ms. Meyers. She said, "Something's going on with Carlie. You need to come in if you can."

Ms. Meyers knew my hectic schedule. She dealt with working mothers all the time, of course, and I was harder to reach than most. She didn't know that I was on my way out at CBS, but she knew I was almost impossible to track down during the school day, so the fact that she was calling me at work was huge. It meant there'd been an emergency of some kind. Otherwise, they would have called Jim or sent home a note. So at first I was panicked that she'd called at all. The teacher thoughtfully explained that Carlie was physically fine, but to please come in and see for myself what was going on. I hung up the phone and thought, *This is my moment to be a superattentive at-home mom.* Here was my chance to swoop in and be there for Carlie. To prove to her why it was so great that I was leaving CBS.

So, I swooped. I dropped whatever I was doing—which was hardly anything—and raced to the school. Ready to beat up the kid who was bullying my little girl, or talk to that kid's parents, or solve the problem, whatever it was. But Carlie needed no such help. Her teacher came out to intercept me in the hallway, and right behind her I could see Carlie, sitting on the floor in front of her classroom door, curled in a knees-up fetal position.

I couldn't imagine what had pushed her to such an unhappy place.

I ran to Carlie's side, and crouched right down on the floor next to her. I was deep into my perfect-mothering moment, determined to pull my daughter through. I said, "Honey, what's wrong? I'm here for you. I came from the newsroom. I heard you were upset, but I'm here now. And it's not just for today. I'll be here all the time now. So tell me, what is it?"

Before Carlie could answer, Ms. Meyers crouched down right next to us and said, "That's actually the problem."

I didn't understand. I said, "What do you mean?"

She said, "Well, Carlie told me you're leaving your job, and she's very upset about it. She's been upset all day."

The whole way up to the school, I'd been trying to imagine what could have been so upsetting to Carlie, my tough little girl. It never occurred to me that it had anything to do with my uncertain job status. I said, "Carlie, honey, this is good news, isn't it? I'm going to be able to spend more time with you."

187

At this, Carlie looked deep into my eyes, almost beseech-ingly, and said, "But Mommy, you love it so much. I don't want you to have to leave."

That moment was the first time I cried over what had hap-pened, what was happening still. My little girl had ripped the veil right off my big lie. She saw so clearly what was simmer-ing below the surface. I was stunned, but immensely proud— that something so wise, so mature, so insightful was coming from the lips of my eight-year-old. There was nothing for me to do but cry. Right there in front of Carlie and her teacher, in the hallway outside their classroom. It was the first time I'd let all those bottled-up emotions about being fired from CBS spill forth. I hadn't mourned what I was losing. I hadn't even let my-self think it through. I'd been so busy trying to be tough and resilient and defiant. It took hearing it from my little girl to make me realize that I was not only lying to my children about what I was facing, but I was also lying to myself.

The great lesson of this exchange, for me, was that kids know. Whatever it is, whatever's going on, they just *know*. Even at eight, Carlie could see that her mother was more than just her mom. She saw what made me tick and thrum. And she knew that my job was more than just a job. She knew there were things about my career at CBS News that defined me, that made me happy—and she wanted me to be able to have those things. It made her sad to think I wouldn't. And it made me sad, too. I also felt terrible for putting her in this position. So at that moment, I stopped lying. I'd tried to cover up what I was feel-ing, and she'd seen right through it. She wanted the truth and deserved it. I realized that this was as good a lesson for my child as any story I could share with her, any intellectual debate we could have around the dinner table, any day at work she might enjoy at my side.

This was life. Mine. Hers. Ours.

From that low moment on, my kids went through the next phase with me. All I could think about at first was finding another job. I was down and despairing for a lot of that time, wondering if I'd ever work again, worrying about money, imagining how I'd fill my days or how I might make some kind of contribution. It was tough, but I shared everything with them. My hopes. My disappointments. Everything. There was a lesson here for my children, I felt sure. A difficult lesson, but one they were ready to hear. When I had a good interview, which was not often, they knew about it. When I had a really bad interview, and started to think I might never get another job, they knew about it. They heard the phone stop ringing, and understood what that meant. They saw my friends—and *theirs*, they'd thought—disappear from our lives, and learned along with me what that meant, too. They watched it all.

Sometimes, parenting is all about sense and feel, and here I had the sense that it was important for them to see me fail and then come out the other side. While my career defined my identity in many ways, I had to learn how to prevent its absence from swallowing me whole. I missed it a lot, and right away. I missed my colleagues and the job we did together. Even today, I still miss many aspects of my time at CBS News. But the lesson of truth amid failure was an important one for me and my children. They've learned to be a little more careful, too. They are wise to how quickly people can rise and fall in my industry, and we take it all a little less seriously together.

I went out on some legendarily bad job interviews. The worst was with CNN's Jon Klein, who quite reasonably wanted to know what had happened at CBS. I couldn't find the words, because no matter how I played it I didn't think he'd believe me. Instead, I stammered my way through some feeble story that didn't come close to answering his question. Plus, I don't think I helped myself in the looks department, either. I felt so down and unsure of myself that I dressed like I had ten years earlier, on *Up to the Minute*. I might as well have written the word "fired" across my forehead, and I walked out of that interview feeling like I'd never work in this business again. To this day I'm angry with myself that I did not sparkle in that interview, that I lost sight of who I was: a reporter, a storyteller, a hard-working mother.

We learned to laugh together as a family at my lowly "unemployed" status, and we encouraged our friends to join us. Consider our tongue-firmly-in-cheek holiday card that year: a shot of Jim and the girls holding signs reading "Please hire her" and "Please give my mommy a job," with me off to the side polishing my nails and holding a bottle of vodka. We were back at it, laughing at the elephant in the room.

Unfortunately, the role of wife and mother didn't even come close to defining me, as my family quickly learned. Once I realized I wasn't about to land a new job anytime soon, I decided to dive right in to being there for my family. Home. Available. I thought I'd take advantage of the situation. Trouble was, I was a terrible cook. And as a housekeeper, I was even worse. I was terrible at folding laundry. I'd fold it, and it would look like someone could have done a better job crumpling it into a ball. I could use the washing machine without too much trouble, but once I took the clothes out of the dryer they were on their own. I couldn't make a bed too well, either—and cleaning and dusting is never too high on my to-do list. Jim was a great sport about my shortcomings in this area. He'd come home and put on an animated voice and say, "Mmmm, something *really* smells good. Has Mommy been making dinner?" He tried, but he just couldn't sell it.

I learned I didn't really have the discipline for the kitchen. I was all thumbs. Always dumping in too much olive oil and turning the heat on too high. Once I cooked a Thanksgiving turkey with the plastic bag filled with gizzards still inside! I was quite capable of *managing* our busy household, but when it came to actually rolling up my sleeves and doing the work, that was a different story. I also found the role of full-time parent tremendously difficult to usurp from Jim—and from the many others who had been helping us out over the years. At one time I'd had to fight myself to give up control over my own children. Now I had to fight to get it back. I had to be the one who made sure they were eating properly, doing their homework, staying on top of their chores. When I was working, I could hide behind the discipline of others; I could be the "fun" mom. The one who took the kids outside to throw water balloons in the street. The one who organized fun adventures with their friends. We could talk about an interesting book my kids were reading, or maybe even read one together, but that's a whole lot different from reading a book for an assignment and helping them write a paper on it. As soon as I had to be the taskmaster, the coordinator of all things domestic, it took some of the spirit out of it. It made it more like a job.

Oh my goodness, it's hard work, being a full-time, stay-at-home mom! Ten times harder than doing a piece for the *CBS Evening News*. I just wasn't up to it, I'm afraid. I have enormous respect for women who can make a go of it at home—men too. My kids saw through me right away. But they humored me. All along, they'd been fairly autonomous, which is how it goes in a house where both parents work. I couldn't even get them to the dentist the first time I tried. I wanted to do all these things for them, even these mundane scheduling things, but Carlie set it up herself. She was about nine, and she was making an appointment on her cell phone because she didn't want to wait for Mommy to get around to scheduling a cleaning. And she had to tell me how to find the dentist's office, too, because I'd never been there before.

Still, I managed to be of some use here and there, and the timing was actually fortunate in a way. Emilie had been developing an eye problem that required some real hands-on therapy and twice-weekly trips to the eye doctor. The treatment went on for months and months, and that time I spent with Emilie was crucial, because it wasn't the sort of thing Jim and I could have entrusted to anyone else. Emilie *did* need me on this. And, happily, I was available, and she is now seeing well and is an honor roll student to boot.

The time at home also turned out to be a blessing on Jim's side of the family. His mother was diagnosed with cancer during this period, and given only months to live. It was so terribly sad, but I was able to take her to a specialist and coordinate her treatments, along with Jim and his brothers. My mother-in-law had always presented a complicated set of challenges for her sons, but here she took on the challenge of fighting her cancer with unbelievable grace. Her bipolar disorder seemed to wash away in the final year of her life—which was in my view her finest moment. She was unyieldingly selfless as she left us. She worried about her sons.

It touched me, and struck me as such a beautiful surprise. Indeed, the very last time I saw my mother-in-law, in hospice care, we had a moment alone and held hands. She pulled me in close and whispered, "Is Jim all right? Will he be okay?"

I remember answering immediately and instinctively, knowing what she was really asking. "Yes," I said. "He *is* all right. He is ready. You have done a good job. You can let go."

She died a week later—and to this day, looking at the kind of man Jim has turned out to be, the kind of husband and father, there is no question "Maw" did a tremendous job. And so here, too, the time at home gave me an enormous gift, one for which I am forever grateful.

All during this period, I thought of how my mother had managed her own transition all those years earlier, when my dad entered the Carter White House. She'd been an artist, pretty much full-time, and all of a sudden she wasn't. Her time was her own, and then it wasn't. It must have been a lot like getting fired, having to step away from what it was that made her who she was. There were times when I was growing up when my parents would move about on edge. There'd be yelling and tension as each worked to get the other to understand. Many of their arguments were about my mother being pulled away from her art and feeling shortchanged. She was at a time in her life when her husband and three kids had to take priority. It was all so *right there* for her, in terms of her art, but because of her role in our family it was also out of reach. She was frustrated, and God bless her for recognizing this, and giving it voice, because it was that fierce determination that drove her back to sculpting. One day it was her turn again. She got her turn because she never lost sight of who she was—and neither did my father.

I worried I'd never get my turn in television again, but I internalized my frustration. I played it all out in my head. Every interview, every prospect, every lead . . . in the beginning, I chased everything. I'd put whatever I was doing on hold and go for it. But that changed, after a while. It had to. It wasn't getting me anywhere, and it was keeping me from the life I *did* have, right in front of me. From time to time, a slim chance at a job would turn up during some important family moment or other. We'd be on vacation, and my agent would call with an interview. Or I'd be working with Emilie on her eye therapy exercises, and I'd see a number on my caller ID that I recognized as a potential lead. But I wouldn't set aside my new role for a mere chance at a return to my old one.

I started telling myself that if they really wanted me, they'd call again. If they didn't . . . well, that was a bad boyfriend I didn't particularly need in my life. That was my new mantra: Don't let your job become the bad boyfriend we've all had, at one time or another. Whatever came next for me, I vowed to recognize this going in, because if you love your job more than it loves you, you'll give it more attention than it's giving you—more attention than it deserves. I didn't want to take a job that would take everything out of me and give nothing back. For a long time, the CBS job was fulfilling and gave back what I put into it, and then some. In the end, however, I let the struggle to stay there consume me. I did not want a repeat of that.

A bad boyfriend job is one you give yourself over to completely, even when there's nothing left to give. Someone you make dinner for when you're not hungry. Someone you make yourself available for, but from whom you ask for no commitment in return. It takes a while, but before long you realize he's just keeping you around until something better comes along. More often than not, that's the merciless reality of being a woman in television news. There is always someone smarter and younger and more eye-catching waiting to take your seat at the table. A bad boyfriend job does not respect you. I'd never exposed myself to such harsh, capricious treatment in my personal life, so why shouldn't my professional life follow the same rules?

In the years since my firing from CBS, I've come to the conclusion that every job in television news is a potential bad boyfriend. A lot of times, women fall into the trap of thinking if they just work really, really hard, and keep really, really focused, that at some point the boyfriend will marry them. But he won't. During my second stint at CBS, starting my first week, with September 11, I tried double-hard to be everything to everybody and got quite far. I let them work me into the ground. And I climbed all the way to the top. But I didn't really take control of who I was and what I was supposed to be. While I had some measure of outward success, my reputation inside CBS was vague and undefined. As soon as new management came in, and the people who'd first *asked me out* were themselves out the door, there was no compelling reason for anyone to keep me around.

And that was on me, in the end.

EIGHT

The Biggest Step Back of All

I DIDN'T KNOW what I was going to do next. Not a clue. For the first time in my career, I could actually imagine a scenario where I wouldn't be able to get another job in television. Every network, every local affiliate from New York to DC had turned me down at least once. I interviewed for great jobs, not so great jobs, and jobs I once would have never considered. Nothing. No leads. No nibbles. One bad interview after another, and each seemed to make the next one worse.

In my head, I kept going back to that bright, shiny penny metaphor I'd carried with me all these years, only now I was a dull, faded wheatback. I had been a shiny penny too many times. I wasn't happy about being out of work, but I was resigned to it. More and more, it was my new reality. Friends kept telling me not to worry, assuring me I'd land another someplace wonderful, sometime soon. Jim tried to pick me up, too. But I couldn't shake the feeling that my time was through. I felt this way most of all in interviews. I kept thinking these television executives were looking right through me. I couldn't quite hold up my end—it was a far cry from when I was being wooed and wowed to re-up at CBS, when I'd made that first splash at MSNBC. When ABC came calling while I was at CBS. I'd gone from fancy lunches and lots of foreplay to being made to wait over an hour outside some nondescript office. I couldn't even get in to see the top executives anymore. I was down to talent recruiters and other lower-level managers. In every way, at every turn, I was feeling older and more obsolete.

I'd been fired by CBS News in a semipublic way, and as the months went by, there was a perception that I was damaged goods. I was always asked. "What happened?" My answers never seemed to suffice, even though I was completely honest. After a while, I tried to put a little positive spin on my firing, or go at it with a self-deprecating sense of humor, but this got me nowhere even faster.

Television news is like any other field in that it's always easier to find a job when you have a job, so I didn't have that going for me, either. The business was changing, too, becoming more fragmented. In the seven years since I'd signed back on with CBS, all kinds of niches had developed—narrowcasting news outlets on cable and on the Web. Entertainment news. Political news. Business news. All produced on the cheap with a lot of pretty young faces out in front. On the one hand, that meant there was a lot of work, because someone had to generate all that new content, but on the other hand, it was the kind of work that could likely be done by entry-level types, young people eager for their first breaks.

Mostly, what I didn't have going for me was the success I'd already achieved. If you're actually open to anything, that's an important message to get across when you're in a very public job market, scratching at despair. Because I'd been working at a fairly high, fairly visible level, people in television invariably thought I would only consider a position at that same level. But I was realistic—I knew I could not start where I'd left off, but I had trouble communicating this to the people who mattered. All I wanted, really, was a job. I met with ABC and NBC. Nothing. CNN . . . nothing. All over town, network and local . . . nothing. I auditioned for a local anchor job in Washington, DC, and came close. But as time went by I started to lose confidence. I was scared we would run out of money. I felt all these pressures, internal and external, real and imagined. All the while, I was trying to convince executives and recruiters that there was nothing wrong with me. But it got to the point where *I* certainly wouldn't have hired me, the way I came across in these meetings.

This went on for months and months. I was depressed—again, not clinically, perhaps, but feeling really, really low. Like I was losing sight of myself. I even applied for a couple of jobs in public relations, thinking the lines between PR and journalism were blurred enough that success in one might lead to success in the other. I'd worked with PR executives throughout my career, so I thought I knew the drill. I could write, pitch, and sell. I actually talked my way into a great PR job, at a top New York firm, but the closer I got to it, the more I realized it wasn't for me. It came with a $300,000 salary, and every time they described what I'd be doing to earn all that money I kept think-

199

ing, *Well, I guess I can do that. It won't be "me"—but yes, I can handle it.*

In the end, I handed that job off to a close friend, a CBS News producer who'd been a part of the Memogate fallout as well. The position really fit her perfectly, whereas with me it would have needed alterations. These nice people at the PR firm actually called me in for my final round of interviews and that was when it hit me. Without thinking twice I said, "That's great, but can I bring along a friend, who might be a better fit?" When my friend called me up a couple of days later to tell me she'd been offered the job, I did question my sanity. But only for a moment. She caught me on my cell phone while I was driving my truck. I pulled over to hear the news. I congratulated her. I was really and truly happy that she had found a perfect fit, and a financial future for her family. But as we spoke, I started banging my head against the steering wheel. I felt like Charlie Brown in those old *Peanuts* strips. I'd been all lined up to kick the football, and then I let Lucy just pull it away at the last moment. In my heart I knew it belonged to my friend and not me. She needed the job and she was ideal for it. I was desperate for a job, but in handing this one off I came a step closer to knowing myself. It was the first time in this mad, frustrating scramble to find a new job that I stopped pushing the fast-forward button to grab at any and every opportunity. The first time I considered the reality of my situation and made a decision that might have been counterproductive in the short term, but absolutely necessary for my long-term health and well-being.

Obviously, this request to bring along my friend struck my PR suitors as peculiar. Unprecedented, really. After all, they were prepared to talk about a deal, and here I was introducing a brand-new candidate to compete for the job I'd applied for in the first place. But I was adamant—that's how convinced I was that this woman would do an absolutely great job. I would not set myself up for a repeat of my disastrous *Up to the Minute* CIA special and just "wing it" for the cash. By the end of the meeting, everyone could see that this former CBS News producer was right for the job, not me.

I realized that television news was my true calling and that it was up to me to do whatever it takes to answer it. Even if it meant starting all over again. I asked my agent to send me out on another round of interviews—this time with talent recruiters and lower-level types. I thought maybe we'd missed something on the first couple passes, by aiming so high.

This new push finally did the trick. Sort of. An ABC News talent recruiter weighed in with a job. It wasn't a particularly good job: anchoring the network's dot.com webcast. I had no idea there even was such a thing, but the woman showed it to me on the in-house monitor and there it was. Like something you'd find at a college television station. It looked as though it was staffed by teenagers. Bad lighting. Bare-bones set. Slapped-together writing. In many ways, it reminded me of *Up to the Minute.* A lot of rip-and-read headlines, pulled directly from the wire services or the network's own news feed. I was just this side of horrified, but knew I had to consider it.

There was nothing else.

I mentioned the webcast prospect to my friend Jim Murphy, the executive producer of *Good Morning America,* who was the executive producer of *CBS Evening News* during my time there. He said, "Just take it, Mika. Get yourself hired. Once you're here at the network, I can use you on *GMA*."

I could do that, I thought. In fact, I *knew* it. But I also knew the job would turn out to be another one of those bad boyfriends. Working ten hours a day on the Web and then weekends at ABC News and maybe mornings on *GMA*, just to prove myself all over again. Another friend at ABC, a vice president, said he could definitely see me getting on *World News Tonight* if I just got myself in the door at the network. The strategy, he said, was to volunteer to work weekends—for no extra pay, of course. Starting all over again didn't scare me, but I was put off by this relationship with ABC from the start. It seemed unhealthy, like I'd be setting myself and my family up for another terrible fall.

I talked myself into taking that job a million times. Then I talked myself out of it a million times more. The salary was ridiculously low, but we needed money. There were no benefits, but Jim had solid medical coverage. I went over all the details in my mind again and again. I'd have to work a ten-hour day, and on top of that try to fit myself in on *Good Morning America*. I'd go from seeing my kids all the time to hardly at all . . . and for what? It was such a skimpy, sketchy prospect, I hated that I was giving it serious consideration. But there I was, giving it serious consideration, even though it seemed like such a jarring shift after all I had put my family through.

I put myself in my mother's shoes. I tried to stand where she had stood during our White House years. Still an artist, just on pause. Not finished. I walked around the ABC newsroom, hoping to get a feel for the place and what a brand-new start there might look like. I knew there'd be opportunities at ABC News, and I knew I could get to every single one. I could definitely be that girl that everyone wanted on their show because she was fast, smart, and always willing to take on an assignment. The shiny penny all over again. I'd impress Charlie Gibson. It was all doable. I was a good writer, a good reporter. I was comfortable anchoring live coverage. I would just have to suck it up. That's the way I had to look at this lowly dot.com job, like it could take me where I wanted to go. Where I needed to go.

So I took it. The dot.com people seemed genuinely surprised and wanted me to start right away. My producer pals were also excited and called me at home to express this. I pretended to be excited, too. They overnighted some contracts and other paperwork for me to sign on a Thursday, and I was due to start the following Monday. It all happened right away. And there I was, sitting at my desk at home that Friday, going over the contract, and unable to sign it. I just physically couldn't do it. I had the pen in my hand, but all I could do was stare at the paperwork. The whole time, there was a voice in my head, trying to talk me into signing: "This is what you have to do, Mika. There's no decision here. No other options. Just take a step back and sign the contract."

Like in the cartoons. A devil on one shoulder, an angel on the other, each pulling in a different direction. "Sign it." "Don't sign it."

I realized it was important and necessary to take a huge step back if I wanted to try and stay in the business. I was mentally there. It had taken almost a year but the message was received. If I truly saw myself as a broadcast journalist, I was going to have to do whatever it took to keep that image alive. Ego, entitlement, and *what people might think* would have to be put aside. It was time to hunker down and start over.

But then, just as I was about to sign, I realized it wouldn't do to take such a fundamental step back unless it was the right step back. And this job just didn't feel right. I put the contract down and called my agent. I wanted to talk it through one more time. But he wasn't interested in listening to me moan about this sorry job. He'd been making calls on my behalf for an entire year, exhausting his Rolodex, and this was the only offer he'd gotten in response. This was where the market was for me. And besides, I'd already agreed to take the job, so I was just spinning everybody's wheels.

I ended up talking things through with one of my agent's associates. She knew me well. She had a good fix on how disappointing this offer must have seemed to me, how dispiriting. She listened well.

"Just do one thing for me," I said, just this side of desperate. "Call MSNBC. One more time. Please. Ask them what they have. Not what they think I would want, but what they have. Press them hard. If you get back nothing, then I'll sign the ABC deal. But I want to know what they have."

My agent's associate said, "Mika, we've been over this. We've been to MSNBC. There's nothing there for you."

I refused to accept that there was *nothing* there for me. Maybe *nothing good*. Maybe *nothing typical*. Or *nothing at my level*. But there had to be something. I said, "I worked there for two years. They know me, and I know them. Before I take this job at ABC, as big a step back as I can take, just call them one more time. Beg, if you have to. Tell them to look in every dark corner of that building for a job, and then come back and tell me what those jobs are. I don't care if it's cleaning toilets."

She said, "Are you sure?"

I said, "I'm not signing this ABC contract. I can't. Just tell MSNBC there's this deal on the table that I'm not at all interested in, and see what they have."

I needed a job, and if I was going to take such a huge step back I would need more control over the situation. The ABC job felt like I would be selling my soul.

Sometimes, the whiff of desperation is what it takes to get things done, because on this last-ditch call my agent's associate managed to get a nibble. A part-time, freelance job, doing cut-ins. At a day rate, on an on-call basis. The MSNBC executive on the other end of the phone was almost afraid to mention it at all, because she felt it was such a step backward. In fact, as soon as she mentioned it, she tried to pull it back. She said, "Mika wouldn't want *that*, would she?"

Cut-ins are the innocuous little "teases" you'll see going into and out of commercial, to get viewers to stay tuned for an upcoming program. At MSNBC, this meant a scripted few headlines, perhaps over accompanying video, promoting *Hardball* or *Scarborough Country* or another one of the network's prime-time shows. I'd be the girl at the fake news desk, saying something forgettable like, "A quick look at what we're working on for you tonight . . ." Then I'd go into a line or two on a developing story, and at the other end I'd say, "And now, back to *Countdown with Keith Olbermann*." Or whatever.

It's a nothing job, really. A space-filler. You sit there. You read the three or four tiny stories they've written out for you. You toss it back to regular programming. A perfectly good assignment for someone just starting out in the business or someone who wants to use it as a stepping-stone. Someone looking to gain her first network exposure. But there'd be nothing exciting about it for me. Nothing creative. Nothing to call on any of the skills I'd developed, covering breaking news and anchoring full-fledged newscasts. In fact, the job I'd had at that very studio eight years earlier was far higher on the totem pole. And the money? A day rate two or three days a week, with no guarantee that they'd use me any more than that, or on anything resembling a regular basis. It was like going from being a partner in a big Manhattan law firm to working as a legal assistant in Poughkeepsie.

I thought it through for about a second. "I'll take it," I said. "Call them back and set it up."

I had my reasons. I knew the culture at MSNBC. I knew how things worked and how they didn't. I knew I could find a way to make myself useful, and that they'd put me to more productive use. And the day-rate aspect of it gave me some power over my own schedule, which I was certain would fill up with requests once my new colleagues saw what I couldn't explain or demonstrate in interviews—that I wasn't damaged goods. Walking in the back door and surprising people would work better for me than trying to impress a network executive in a job interview. The public relations job would have offered a healthy paycheck right away, and the chance to work at a fairly high level with predictable hours, but I would have failed at it. That, I couldn't do. The ABC job would have paid more than this part-time cable position, but it was full-time *plus* from the start. That, I couldn't do either. But this cut-in gig at MSNBC . . . this I could do. In my sleep. And it offered a lot more upside than any of the other prospects. It was a step back, but it was not a bad boyfriend.

As soon as I accepted the job, I felt myself coming back to life, as if I'd received a transfusion. It was amazing, really, considering the position I'd held at CBS, up against the one I was about to take at MSNBC. But during that full year and more that I was out of work, I discovered who I was and what I was meant to do, regardless of my assignment or my annual salary. I discovered what my terms would be this time around. And as I recharged, I knew I was making the right decision. I remember going out to dinner with Jim and his producer the night I took the job, and I was terrifically excited. I loved having a plan, having someplace to go in the morning. My friends were all stunned at my self-imposed fall from grace. But it didn't matter that some in the industry would ridicule my job once word got around that my career had been downsized by such a significant degree. This wasn't about *them*. This was about me. Bottom line: it put me back to work. It allowed me to get back in my car and drive to a newsroom and flash my ID and hear that little beep go off so I could be waved inside. It gave me back a sense of my professional self—in a part-time way, to start, which meant I could keep some of that work-family balance I'd been building for the previous year. With the possibility of more responsibilities to come.

During all this time at home I had started to feel like I didn't have anything to offer the girls. I wanted my daughters to have everything they could possibly have in this life. Not in terms of material things, but in terms of being full. Using every talent, making room for whatever it was that gave them joy and purpose. I wanted them to access all of it in themselves. But they weren't seeing that from me lately. They weren't seeing me involved or engaged at home or at work in a way that made me sparkle and look forward to the next day with great hope and possibility. I was losing my identity and starting to think that if I couldn't present myself as a positive role model to my own daughters then I was failing miserably as a mother. That if I wasn't *full* they'd see me as empty.

Once again, I pictured my own mother, negotiating some of these same issues when I was about the same age as my daughters. If I closed my eyes, I could see myself back on our farm in Virginia, marveling at the sudden turn our lives had taken. I could hear my mother's plaintive arguments with my father: "You get to go and run the world, but what do I get? I'm just driving the children around all day. I love you all, but I need some time to do my art."

That's how I was starting to feel. Like I was just driving my kids around all day. I love my beautiful children. And I have great respect for parents who find their joy and purpose in being there for their children in a full-time way. I envy their ability to draw such nobility and validity from that extraordinarily important role. But it wasn't me. I tried. I even went to the dog park every morning and made an effort to hang with the other moms after we'd sent our kids off to school. I started helping with school fundraisers and found myself stuffing envelopes at a kitchen table with four women from my town. But my focus was elsewhere. Halfway into the project, I got the MSNBC job and disappeared. It felt like I was escaping. For months, I would see one of the envelope-stuffers in town and run in the other direction, embarrassed at my pathetic effort at being a fundraiser.

I'd missed being out on the road, like when I drove up to Portland, Maine, to chase down a last-minute lead on a long investigative piece about faulty ball joints on the Dodge Durango. My producer Betty Chin and I had done several follow-up reports on this story, when someone from Portland sent an e-mail with another faulty ball-joint lead to round out our series. We dropped what we were doing and headed north in my pickup truck. We drove the whole way jabbering about the story. We had a cameraman meet us there and set the whole thing up on the fly. We ended up landing this great visual element to our piece that ultimately cost Chrysler millions in a nationwide recall, because they'd been putting out these faulty ball-joints. We were up and back in a day, exhausted but exhilarated. *Those* were the types of days I missed most of all. Being invigorated by the story, the storytelling, the process of collaborating with bright minds to bring it all together. Never knowing what was around the next bend. Finding the story in the unlikeliest places. Putting it on the air and making some kind of difference. What it came down to was having someplace to go in the morning other than the dog park.

Meanwhile, as I expected, I was ridiculed by my former colleagues for taking such a big step back in my career. As it turned out, that big open wound was a little deeper than I'd imagined. I had so much time on my hands between cut-ins, I started going online and reading all the negative chatter being posted on news sites. Really hateful stuff . . .

Look what Mika has become.
What a fall from grace.
She must be so desperate.
Poor thing.
Did she have plastic surgery while she was gone?

There was an endless stream of gossip and vitriol, most of it posted by my former colleagues and friends. Who else would take the time to write about something like this? No one cares as much about television news as the people who work in television news—and here I was, trying to find my professional footing and getting tripped by the same people I'd counted on at one point in my career. All I could do was put a smile on my face, keep my head down, and go back to work.

The job itself wasn't bad. My photo was still hanging in the MSNBC lobby in Secaucus, New Jersey, from my first, much-higher-profile stint at the network. The same security guard was there, more than six years later. On my first day back, he said, "Hi, Mika." Then, "Ummm . . . Mika?" As if he was trying to remember if I'd really left.

The makeup and hair people were mostly the same, which was fun and wonderful because the MSNBC team is the best in the business. Everywhere I looked, there were recognizable faces. This was a good thing and a not so good thing. Good, because I felt comfortable immediately, in such familiar surroundings. Not so good, because I had to explain to all these people what the hell I was doing there in such a diminished role.

In all, I worked a four-hour shift. Prime time. Two or three nights a week. I was responsible for one or two cut-ins per hour. No more than two or three minutes each, reading from someone else's script, so I didn't even have to write my own material. It was such a mindless, one-hand-tied-behind-my-back sort of job that I got bored pretty quickly. So easy it hurt. I used to do our household bills between reports, or talk to my friends on the phone, or help my kids with their homework. Anything to amuse myself and fill the time. It felt to me like I was punching a clock, but I had a handle on it mentally. This was not a bad boyfriend at all. Rather, I considered MSNBC a very comfortable old boyfriend. There wasn't the thrill of chasing down one of those ball-joint-type moments of discovery, but I liked that I was good at this one small thing. I had the self-assurance to know the next job would come soon enough. I took the time to ease my children into our new routines at home. They had a working mommy again, and we talked about those changes, so there'd be no surprises.

I made it a special point not to rush to make friends at MSNBC. I didn't make a big deal about going back to work. I just enjoyed contributing to the household income and being useful in a field that I loved. I steered clear of my old ways of rushing through each day and taking on more than I could reasonably handle. I wanted to take a moment during this step

back to breathe, to remember who I was and what was important—and not to make the same mistakes again.

After just a couple of weeks, things started to happen without my even pushing it or asking. The network needed someone to do an hour, middle of the afternoon. Was I available?
Then, another hour. And another. They kept putting me out
there, hosting newscasts throughout the day, because they
knew I could do the job. No one stopped to remember that I'd
hosted a three-hour show eight years earlier at this very same
network, and that this was like riding a bike to me. But this time
I wasn't impressed with myself or my bosses. This was my second run at MSNBC, and I expected things would play out just
like they had during my second run at CBS. The bright, shiny
penny feeling would start to dull, and I would lose my gleam,
and knowing this and being okay with it was the most liberating aspect of what was happening. I was able to host for hours
and hours with confident live skills, calling on more than
twenty years of experience and, now, something else: no fear.
It was like skiing down a well-groomed intermediate slope on
a beautiful day, instead of snowshoeing uphill in a blizzard. I
was earning the same day rate, but the windfall was that it came
with a little more self-respect and empowerment. The behind-
the-back sneers stopped. The snide comments online fell away.
The murmuring in the hall as I walked past . . . gone. I started
to get hosting work every day, and calls began coming in from
NBC Nightly News—part of the same corporate family, the
same news division.

I thought, *Here we go again.* I was asked to do an NBC
News special report and my bosses thought I nailed it. I remem-

ber taking their reaction as a backhanded compliment. I had done hundreds of these reports for CBS, but I guess in the news business no one remembers anything unless it happened in the past five minutes. This, too, was a liberating realization. I'd come back in at the bottom, and I would continue to pleasantly surprise my bosses. And this time I wouldn't have to reach *all the way* to the top, I told myself. Just a little higher. It'd be far better even, I thought, to grab at something *new*. Something I *hadn't* done.

I had no idea what was in store, but I was open to anything.

And then, on April 4, 2007, syndicated CBS Radio personality and MSNBC morning host Don Imus cracked a tasteless joke during the NCAA women's basketball tournament. He described the Rutgers University women's basketball team as "nappy-headed hos," and set in motion a controversial sequence of events that would change the landscape at MSNBC, where his morning radio program had been simulcast since 1996. Soon, the network was scrambling to fill the *Imus in the Morning* time slot, which had been the station's signature show for over ten years. As soon as Imus was fired, there was a mad scramble. Every MSNBC host and news personality wanted in. It was like a good old-fashioned land grab, with all these different, competing interests trying to stake out their new territory.

I looked on in a bemused sort of way, because it didn't really affect me. It meant there was more airtime to fill in general, so it's possible some of that would fall to me. But it also threw the entire network lineup into question. One day I bumped into Joe Scarborough, the former Florida congressman who hosted one of the prime-time hours I'd been plugging as part of my job. I saw him during one of my cut-in shifts.

He spoke first. He introduced himself and said, "Hi Mika, great to meet you, even if you make fun of my show everynight."

This caught me off guard. I had no idea what he was talking about—until I remembered that I often tossed back to *Scarborough Country* with a mock emphasis on its name. I tried to finesse my way out of it. I said, "How can I make fun of a show that I never watch?"

He laughed, realizing I was having some fun at his expense. But he didn't seem to mind. He was nice, gracious. After a beat he said, "Do you want to do a show with me tomorrow morning? They're trying me out in the Imus spot. I need someone to sit next to me and make conversation."

My first thought was to decline. It was my second thought, too. I was working until eleven o'clock that night. The last thing I wanted was to get up at three o'clock in the morning and hustle back out to Secaucus to help this guy audition for Imus's time slot. So I said, "I'm sorry, Joe. I'll have to pass. I'm working late. You wouldn't want me on the set with no sleep."

But Joe wouldn't take no for an answer. He kept at it. He knew what he wanted for his show. Mostly, he knew what he *didn't* want—a bubble-headed chickadee as his newsreader and cohost. Right away, he could tell that I might bring a little edge to the table. Unlike most men in television news, he saw my edge and fortysomething age as assets for *Morning Joe*—he already had the name. He was putting together his on-air team, and thirty seconds after meeting me he got it in his head that

I would be a part of it. He knew he'd need some kind of side-kick or sounding board to make a morning show work on the network, and decided I'd be a good fit. Just like that. And so he started calling management. No one on high at MSNBC could quite see in me what Joe Scarborough saw in me, but they finally relented and offered me a few shifts on the morning show audition process.

I didn't know much about Joe. I wasn't lying when I said I'd never seen *Scarborough Country*. But I knew he was sharp, and quick on his feet, and good on camera. I knew he was a conservative Republican, which I found interesting. I welcomed the prospect of a few heated, all-out debates on politics and society. Still, I wanted no part of that morning time slot. Once in a while, a few shifts here and there . . . that was fine. It showed that I was a team player. But I had a nice little thing going: just a few weeks into my born-again stint at MSNBC, I was filling in regularly on the 3 PM show. Then I'd do my cut-ins and go home. No stress. No hassle. No being all things to all people. Why would I want to get up with the roosters and come in at such a ridiculous hour? And why would I drag myself through such a public audition?

But Joe was persistent, I'll say that. He finally wore me down enough to audition. I wasn't committing to anything just yet, and neither was MSNBC. They were wheeling in a whole mess of different hosts, trying to decide how to fill that spot. It wasn't Joe's yet, but he was operating as if it were a done deal. I didn't trust his certainty, although I admired his confidence. But then again I'd been through this many times before, at this very network. Even at CBS, before they landed Katie Couric,

Newsweek had put me on its list as a "dark horse" candidate for a co-anchor job. And I'd been at the center of all that buzz during my big *60 Minutes* promotion. I had been there and done that and no longer felt the need to expose myself or my kids to more of the same ups and downs. Mostly the *downs*, I'll admit, but at this stage in my life and career, even the *ups* had me worried. Just thinking about it made me very, very tired.

Joe Scarborough, "Morning Joe," had no such reservations. He was going to grab this moment and bring me along for what would become a fascinating and groundbreaking journey.

NINE

Finding My Voice

SOMETIMES THE BIGGEST BREAKS come from the smallest chance encounters. If there was ever a fortune-cookie-worthy sentiment to emerge from the arc of my career, this would be it. Joe says it took him all of five seconds to spot me as his future co-host. He liked my "snarkiness." He liked that I seemed to regard the current television news landscape as a little bit boring, a little bit *yesterday*. He had already seen me on the air, so he knew I could carry a newscast, but as soon as he met me he saw that I could carry a conversation as well. This was key. And it was something I didn't know men in television were seeking from their female colleagues. Most of them were looking "at" something, not "for" something. I wasn't about to argue with him. But I wasn't about to drop everything and sign on to his audition, either.

Joe had some big ideas for this morning show, but I didn't want to hear them. It was a *morning* show, after all. I hated the morning shift. So no ideas could turn me around—unless the plan was to tape the thing at a reasonable hour. On a one-shot basis, though, I would agree to almost anything. I didn't mind coming in early a time or two just to help this affable, extremely persuasive colleague see if he could gain any support for his show. At the same time, I would be putting it out there to the MSNBC brass that I was a team player, willing to answer the call—even at such an ungodly hour.

He set the whole thing up. We had three hours to fill, and as far as I knew Joe had no real game plan. What I didn't know was that he had already figured out how he was going to spend each minute of those three hours. His plan was to turn the standard three-minute "talking head" interview into a twenty-minute discussion. We would toss out celebrity gossip and focus on hard news—becoming, Joe believed, the must-see destination for policy-makers and media leaders. The on-air chemistry was essential; the conversation needed to be organic. I was skeptical until our first day when that red light went on. Something clicked. Something I had never seen before in twenty years of being on television. Within twenty-five seconds, I was sold. We gave our take on the news of the day, venting on what needed venting and talking about what interested *us*, not management or a many-headed team of producers. There was just one producer in charge, Chris Licht, who would often interact with us on the air.

I'd worked with many co-anchors over the course of my career, but this was different. The rapport between me and Joe was easy, natural, completely unforced. It was as if we had been friends for years. It's true I'd been on the set with Dan Rather,

Ed Bradley, and Bob Schieffer. I'd worked with some of the biggest eight-hundred-pound gorillas in the business. But here, we moved easily in and out of complex discussions. Right away, I could see what Joe was after and that we would be the antidote for people who were tired of typical television fare—people like us. I was so busy looking for a job over the past year, I hadn't tapped in to one of the reasons I had been so down about my prospects—namely, that the business has become redundant and cheap and predictable. But when Joe and I got going, we were determined to go at it in an unvarnished way, to say whatever came to mind. To ask questions the viewers at home might actually want to know the answers to. Each of us had been up and down in our respective careers, and that added to our texture. We were unafraid, and willing to work without the mountain of preproduction notes that can be so suffocating on a news set.

Yes, this was still an audition. Technically. The plug could have been pulled on us at any moment, but we didn't care. I have to hand it to our boss, Phil Griffin, for letting our show gel, naturally. I never knew what Joe would say next, which in turn meant I never knew what I'd say next, but I felt safe and comfortable. I was having a blast. It continued to surprise me that this was the type of television I'd never done before, the type of television I'd never seen.

I was wading into the world of "opinion television" and political analysis. Joe Scarborough was an expert at this, so I was lucky to learn from one of the very best. And lucky to try something new at this late, born-again stage in my career. To challenge myself intellectually. I wasn't flying completely blind. I

219

had my finely honed diplomatic skills, developed over the years at the family table and our eclectic Brzezinski dinner parties. I had my twenty-plus years of television news experience. And I had an open mind. I was up for anything, as long it was interesting, and this was certainly interesting. So interesting that before we'd gotten through our first half-minute on the air, I caught myself thinking, *Watch out, Mika. This guy is fearless. And supremely talented. This show could be a winner.* And then I checked myself and thought, *No, it* will *be a winner.* I was dead solid certain. Sold.

All we needed was a green light from the network and we'd be good to go. Unfortunately, it took MSNBC a while to figure it out. To figure *us* out. They were still auditioning all these different hosts to fill that Imus slot. This went on for weeks and weeks. I told myself I didn't mind the hours, because it was still just a speculative deal. No reason to turn my life upside down just yet. I'd suck it up, put my body clock on snooze, and sprint ahead. I was still working on a freelance basis, still filling in on other shows. Still very much up in the air.

By June 2007, it was decided that *Morning Joe* would be slotted as a permanent part of the MSNBC schedule, in the abandoned Imus spot. This was great news, only I wasn't made a permanent part of the package at first. I was still working on a freelance basis, and management was still free to assign me to fill in all across the MSNBC lineup. I'd be tethered to the *Morning Joe* set for the time being, but there were no guarantees. I had no choice but to accept my uncertain status, yet I couldn't understand it, especially after the show became a hit and started to make some noise in political circles in Washington and all across the country. Despite our promising start, management was not convinced about my future on the show.

I should mention here that there was no real incentive for MSNBC to attach me in a long-term way to *Morning Joe*. As far as I know, it was never even discussed. I was most valuable to the network in the bullpen, where they could call on me in a pinch. I was a relatively inexpensive hire. A stopgap, really. I understood that. That loose setup might have continued indefinitely, but for another one of those small chance encounters. This time, it was an unlikely run-in over Paris Hilton that pushed my career to an unexpected place.

MSNBC had just relaunched *Morning Joe* as a fixture of its lineup. They were starting to promote us. We were beginning to develop a following. I was working hard booking big-name guests through my contacts made at CBS and our connections. I was beginning to invest in *Morning Joe* in a big way.

Willie Geist had been added to our anchor desk, and the three of us had quickly fallen into a relaxed, interesting rapport. Here, at last, was that right mix of people Joe had been seeking. We still had our own take on the news and on politics. And we still made it up as we went along, using our gut as a basis for the political discussions. In this way, the show more closely resembled a talk radio show than a television talk show. We talked about what was going on in our lives, in our neighborhoods, in the world at large. Mostly about politics, but there was room for everything else. Whatever we wanted to talk about.

Whatever was going on in the world. We didn't spend too much time worrying about the visuals. It was the conversation that mattered.

I felt like I was back at the Brzezinski family dinner table, fighting to make myself heard. Technically, Willie and I were "co-hosts," supporting players to Joe, but that was just fine with me. In fact, I felt it was exactly where I belonged. Again, this was part of knowing who I was—and I was finally getting the idea. For years, I had been filled with the Kool-Aid. Always a little too inclined to believe whatever these network executives had to say to me about my bright, promising future. Always urged to go for the biggest job, to be number one, to land that promotion. But a supporting role is actually more suited to my personality. It's a better fit. There was one problem, though. The assignment was beginning to feel like another one of those bad boyfriend setups, because I was being tapped to do so many other things besides *Morning Joe. Nightly News* pieces. Hosting multiple dayside hours, after our show wrapped. Filling in as newsreader on *Weekend Today* all the while booking guests and candidates for *Morning Joe*, helping the show get on the map.

Sound familiar?

It's like there were two trains running on my career track. The *Morning Joe* line, and the freelance, pinch-hitting line. I found myself hoping the *Morning Joe* train would get in ahead of schedule, and I could devote my full attention to it before long, but for the time being it was a dual commitment. We offered our opinions freely on the *Morning Joe* set—and we came at these stories from such different perspectives that it almost always made for attention-grabbing television. What I liked was that we didn't put on a typical newscast—which at this point in my career would have really felt like acting. We said what we really thought, even if it cut against television news convention. We were transparent. The only aspect of our show that was "preproduced" or slick-packaged in any way was the news segment that I would read at the top and bottom of every hour. Those headline-type stories were written for us, and the scripts were usually handed to me at the last minute and I would read them cold—in a *this just in* sort of way.

On this one morning, the lead story put me in a tailspin. Paris Hilton was released from prison. That was the lead. I couldn't believe it. How amazingly insipid, I thought. And it got my back up. I had no problem discussing Paris Hilton's release on our show. It rated a mention—but only as a kind of footnote. Or maybe as a punch line. It was a big story that June—but an inconsequential story to me. The surprise, as I started my cold read, was that our news writer was running with it as our lead. His thinking was that our accompanying video was something "fresh," because it had been taken from her midnight release from prison. That meant it had not yet been plastered all across the cable news channels. People would be tuning in and seeing it on our show for the first time. But it also meant we were ignoring a far bigger story.

Richard Lugar, the Republican senator from Indiana, had just broken with President Bush on the war in Iraq, and that should have been our headline. No question. We'd already gotten into it at the top of the show, so I just assumed I'd read the straight story once we hit our first news break. Very often, that's how it would work. We'd talk around an issue or a developing story, and then I'd go at it again in a straight report during our news segment. I quite reasonably assumed that's what would happen here on this morning, because there was nothing screaming across the wires or from the day's newspapers to suggest otherwise. This was a big deal, and it should have been the lead.

But as I looked at the monitor, I got an eyeful of our get-out-of-jail-free video of Paris Hilton, which was meant to roll while I read the story that was now flashing on my teleprompter. I only had a couple of seconds to process everything, and in that time Joe was wrapping up our top-of-the-show chatter, and he could see that something was bothering me. I wasn't quite fuming, but I was steamed. He finished his thought about Senator Lugar, then turned to me and said, "Mika, what's in the news?"

Like he always did.

Like he continues to do.

In response, I said something like, "Well, Joe, you'd think that would be our top story, wouldn't you?" Meaning Senator Lugar's about-face.

I hadn't meant to say anything, but out it came. To this day, I can't say what came over me. My buttons had been pushed in this way before, and I'd always maintained my professionalism. Always done my job. Few questions asked—unless you count the ones I might have mumbled under my breath. But this show was different. Being brutally honest was the essence of what we were doing. And so I became incensed that I was being asked to report such a frivolous item at the top of our newscast, when there was a story of real moment and importance to consider. I was supposed to sell the Paris story as interesting. To me, though, it was emblematic of everything that was wrong with television news. The conflation of news and entertainment. The pandering to the lowest common denominator. The puffing-up of socialites and non-starter celebrities who had somehow collected a measure of fame just by being famous. It set me off, that I was being asked to read such a nothing story on a morning when there was so much else going on.

So I didn't. I refused to read the teleprompter. I set down my script and told my new colleagues that I couldn't read this item and pass it off as news.

Joe and Willie knew good television when they saw it. So the two of them started egging me on. Baiting me. But I wouldn't bite. I didn't care if they fired me over this. My one abiding thought was, *Look, I'm forty years old, and I've been doing this a long time, and I can't pretend that this is news.* It might *look* like news. It might *feel* like news. It might even *smell* like news. But it certainly wasn't news, and I made my position plain. I guess that's what happens when you wander through the wilderness of a long career. Somewhere along the way, you're bound to figure out who you are. What you stand for. What's important. And what's not.

In a flash, I thought back to the segments I'd been asked to report when I was anchoring the overnight newscast for CBS. I used to watch those tapes while I was out of work, trying to figure out where things went wrong, all the time thinking, *Goodness, Mika, you were such a fake. Such a poser.* Vacation-planning tips? Coupon-clipping strategies? Bras that make you feel good *and* look good? (Imagine *that!*) I presented all of it as if it had some earth-shattering importance. I watched that material again and thought, *I'm just not interested.* And do you know what? Most women aren't interested, either. I'm sorry. They're not. They're being force-fed this crap on morning television—and this Paris Hilton story just jumped out at me as the latest example of more of the same.

Once again, the notion ran through my head that I could be fired over something like this. But I didn't care. I thought, *You know what? Fire me. Go ahead. Like I'm scared of that happening again.* And underneath that thought was another: *This feels good.* I stepped outside myself for a beat and felt like the actress in those old shampoo commercials, the one who was just so darn pleased with the bounce and luster and fullness of her hair that she couldn't help but shout, "Yes! Oh, yes!"

I kept quiet, but in my head I was shouting, *Oh, yes!*

And that might have been that. Except it wasn't. Joe wouldn't let it go. Willie wouldn't let it go. At the top of the hour, when the news came around again, the Paris Hilton story was right where I'd left it. In the lead. Top of the pile. Page one. It was almost a joke. So I tried to light my script on fire. Willie stopped me, a heads-up, safety-first-type move, so I just tore it up instead.

At the next news break, I called for a paper shredder, and vowed that if the story bounced back to me a third time I would feed it through. At this point, we had lapsed into performance art, and it was a great performance, and I was determined to make a statement. An important statement, I believed. We were all having fun with it. Sure enough, they tried to get me to read

the story again, right up top, so I was true to my word: I shred-
ded it. We got some good discussion out of it, and some laughs,
and then we moved on to other, more salient things. Before I
knew it, our three hours were up. It felt like a solid show, but
nobody thought anything of it, really. It was just one show in
a long string of many. We'd done our thing, and when we were
out of time we said our good-byes and figured we'd go at it
again the next day.

I went home and took a nap. That was my routine in the
early days of *Morning Joe,* when I was still adjusting to the
schedule. Business as usual. I needed my sleep—and I tended
to grab it before my kids got home from school. I was out for
maybe twenty minutes before my BlackBerry started vibrating.
I ignored it at first, in a back-of-my-dreams sort of way. I heard
it and I didn't, all at the same time. Then I heard it and I didn't
again. Finally, on the tenth or twentieth or thirtieth call, the
noise managed to pierce through that thin veil of sleep and
shake me awake. The red light was flashing, flashing, flashing.
I picked up the phone and saw a long list of e-mails and missed
calls. Hundreds of them. Ultimately, thousands. All lined up and
clamoring for immediate attention. The BBC, requesting an interview. Viewers who had somehow spelled my name correctly
and managed to surmise my e-mail address. Someone from the
NBC press office, wanting to know if I would appear on Nether-
lands television, on Australian television, on National Public
Radio. I'm surprised my BlackBerry didn't implode from the
weight of all those messages—all of them extremely positive.
People thanked me for pointing out the ridiculous tension between hard news and entertainment news. For taking a stand.

People cheered me on. Told me to keep it going. Someone called me the bravest woman in journalism. It was "the shred heard around the world," according to one e-mail. Before long, there was a clip of that morning's show on YouTube, and not too long after that it had been seen by more than a million people. Then, two million. Then, three . . . then, four.

The response meant our show was on the map, and our voice had been defined in that one moment of morning show defiance. And it was a voice that people wanted to hear.

The calls and e-mails kept coming for the next several weeks. The requests for interviews. It was the very definition of viral, and I was still trying to process what exactly it was that I had done, except be true to myself. I was stormed by surprise. The thing took on a life of its own. MSNBC executives were thrilled. Our show was still brand-new, and this was our first public confirmation that we were onto something—all because of a silly, nothing moment that came about because I'd refused to read a silly, nothing story.

It was bigger than any of us could have imagined. Before that first week was out people were stopping my dad on the street, asking him if he was related to Mika Brzezinski from MSNBC's *Morning Joe.* That had never happened before. They asked my brothers, too. Also a first. My mother was smart enough to recognize it for what it was—just a whole lot of fuss over a whole lot of nothing. But it struck a chord. It really did. It set us off on a positive path. It even pushed the folks at MSNBC to give me a show of my own, about a week later. An hourlong show at 9 AM, right after *Morning Joe*—*MSNBC Live with Mika Brzezinski.* That lasted just a couple of months, before we all realized what we had with *Morning Joe,* and that perhaps I might be diluting "the Joe and Mika brand" by being on the air for that extra hour, reporting on missing girls and trench collapses that we normally wouldn't touch on our flagship show.

Our success didn't push MSNBC to give me a full-time *Morning Joe* contract, though. That wouldn't happen for another year—and only after I demanded it or this bad boyfriend would be history. I actually used the term when I walked into Phil Griffin's office. I said, "This job is becoming a bad boyfriend. You need to marry me or the relationship is over." To the network's great credit, they came through. I'd reached the point in my up-and-down-and-now-up-again career where a network executive had actually referred to "the Joe and Mika brand" in discussing my work. I heard those words and smiled, because I knew full well that my *brand* had been through the ringer a time or two. And, in all likelihood, it would be put through a few times more before it was all over. I thought about how far I'd come, from a teeny tiny station in Vermont; to a wee-hours paper-pushing stretch behind the scenes at ABC; to local, siren-chasing stints in Hartford and New Haven; to a local anchor seat that briefly cast me as Connecticut's sweetheart and presumptive mother-of-the-year; to a graveyard shift disappointment at CBS News, where I tried to do too much, too soon, on too little sleep; to a fledgling afternoon cable show that happened to launch eighteen months before an ever-breaking election story of such historical significance it would change the face of daytime news programming; back again to CBS and another monumental story that would establish me as a go-to correspondent and rising star, or so I thought; to a sudden fall from grace that left me reeling and out of work for over a year; to the mother of all steps back and a return to cable, as a day-rate part-timer, doing lowly cut-ins . . . all the way to our upstart morning show that was poised to get out of the gate in a big-time way.

Like I said, I'd struck gold with *Morning Joe.* I suppose I knew that on one level, which was why I was getting up so early in the morning those first few weeks, but it took this curious little standoff over Paris Hilton for me to recognize it in a full-on way. I thought back to my first big contract at CBS. It was for more money than I'd ever imagined. I was so happy I went out and bought myself a diamond necklace to celebrate. It wasn't like me to make such an extravagant purchase. But there would be no treats this time around. No extravagance. The job itself would be my diamond necklace. My present . . . to me.

The gift is the challenge. The opportunity. The chance to try on an entirely new role and find that I was born to it.

Jump ahead to where I am today. Where *we* are today. *Morning Joe* has become must-see TV for political junkies, setting the agenda for the day for much of the media world. We have found a place for our voices and opinions. Whether Democrats or Republicans disagree with our take on an issue, it never stops them from appearing on our show. We have questioned every decision made by President Barack Obama, only to be invited to broadcast our show live from the White House.

It was a show from the lawn outside the West Wing, in the middle of winter. The sub-zero temperatures had me thinking somebody was trying to kill us, until the last segment. Chris

Licht had worked the phones throughout the whole show and got us an unprecedented live tour of the West Wing, with Press Secretary Robert Gibbs. I couldn't feel my feet, but the segment was exhilarating and made news.

We stand now on the front lines, the future of television news—absolutely not where I expected to be the day I walked out of CBS, on my thirty-ninth birthday, certain my career had come to an end.

This wasn't all my doing, of course. A lot of it was hardly my doing. But I was a part of it. A big part. And that part would have never happened if I hadn't held true to every facet of my personality. Mother, wife, journalist. All things at once, just like my mother had tried to get me to understand in that *Sunday Morning* piece. Knowing that it was still in me, even when it was taken away, gave me the confidence to take that giant step back. Knowing that I had nothing to lose but a sense of self-importance gave me the strength of character and the good, common sense to take that giant step forward—and helped to set the tone for our show. All along, there was no promise that I'd be able to work my way back into the mix, except the promise that I made to myself. To do whatever it took. To keep life and career in focus and in perspective, just like my mother had been able to do with her art for those four long White House years.

As my first year on *Morning Joe* came to an end, it was obvious that I had become part of something special. Happily, my bosses at NBC agreed, and rewarded me with a new contract and a full-time assignment to *Morning Joe*.

Our holiday card that year was a shot of Jim and the girls with our babysitter. I'm not in the picture at all. The inscription: "If you see Mommy, please wish her a Merry Christmas."

I was on the road much of the time—but this assignment kept us in balance. This time we had it covered. This time Jim and the girls were all proud and on board and had the feeling that Mommy was more "there" than ever before. This time we all had a clear sense of who I was, what I could handle—and where we were going as a family.

I am closer today to fully embracing my mother's lesson—to holding all things at once dear to your heart. There is no reason to tie a bow on this story because that would be a lie. Our days are often grueling trying to juggle it all. But today, Carlie is a fabulous rider and student and no worse for the wear after that terrible fall eleven years ago and Emilie is an honor roll student who runs on the track team like a gazelle. Tomorrow will hold new challenges and changes and choices. For Jim and me, the girls are our gauge as we make decisions by the day on how to balance everything at once.